Quick knits to wear™

Edited by Jeanne Stauffer

Exclusively using Brown Sheep yarns

HOUSE of
WHITE
BIRCHES
PUBLISHERS
SINCE 1947

Quick Knits to Wear

Editor: Jeanne Stauffer

Art Director: Brad Snow

Publishing Services Manager: Brenda Gallmeyer

Associate Editor: Dianne Schmidt

Copy Supervisor: Michelle Beck

Copy Editors: Conor Allen, Mary Martin

Technical Editor: Diane Zangl

Technical Artist: Chad Summers

Book & Cover Design: Karen Allen

Graphic Artist Supervisor: Ronda Bechinski

Graphic Artist: Debby Keel, Jessi Butler

Production Assistant: Cheryl Kempf, Marj Morgan

Photography Supervisor: Tammy Christian

Photography: Matt Owen

Photography Assistant: Tammy Nussbaum

Chief Executive Officer: John Robinson

Publishing Director: David Mckee

Book Marketing Director: Craig Scott

Editorial Director: Vivian Rothe

Publishing Services Director: Brenda R. Wendling

Printed in China

First Printing: 2005

Library of Congress Number: 2004105976

Hardcover ISBN: 1-59217-059-5

Softcover ISBN: 1-59217-066-8

Every effort has been made to ensure the accuracy and completeness
of the instructions in this book. However, we cannot be responsible for
human error or for the results when using materials other than those
specified in the instructions, or for variations in individual work.

All photos taken at Swiss Heritage Village, Berne, Indiana.

A Note From the Editor

In 1980, Harlan Brown, owner and founder of Brown Sheep Company, Inc. fulfilled his dream of spinning his own yarn, using the wool from his own sheep. Harlan had farmed his grandfather's beloved western Nebraska farm for 35 years, and now he was ready to take the next step. The first year was dedicated to perfecting one line of yarn, what is known today as Top of the Lamb. Since that time, he has developed many yarns in a wide array of colors, giving the hand knitter more choices than ever!

Miles away in northeast Indiana, a second generation of printers were looking to expand their business, so they purchased a publishing company, House of White Birches. Initially, the company only published magazines, but before long, they were publishing books of all sizes in many different interest areas, including knitting.

Because of the history of both companies, we shot all the photographs in this book at Swiss Heritage Village. This historical village provided the perfect background for the easy-to-knit ponchos, cardigans, jackets, summer tops, shawls, scarves, hats, etc. In this collection, you'll find designs are funky and flashy, chic and sleek or timeless and refined. Many of the garments have classically simple lines, yet retain a certain flair that makes them trendy. But no matter what the style you prefer, you'll love knitting these projects using the gorgeous yarns from Brown Sheep Co.

Warm regards,

Jeanne Stauffer

Contents

Chunky Turtleneck Tunic

Design by Bonnie Franz

A touch of color adds spark to a chunky Aran-style pullover.

Skill Level

EASY

Size

Woman's extra-small (small, medium, large, extra-large) Instructions are given for smallest size, with larger sizes in parentheses. When only 1 number is given, it applies to all sizes.

Finished Measurements

Chest: 35 (39, 43, 47, 51) inches
Total length: 27½ (28, 28¼, 28¼, 29) inches
Sleeve length: 16½ (17, 17, 17, 17¼) inches

Materials

- Brown Sheep Burly Spun 100 percent wool super bulky yarn (132 yds/8 oz per hank): 4 (5, 5, 5, 6) hanks cream #BS10 (MC), 1 hank fuchsia #BS23 (CC)
- Size 13 (9mm) needles or size needed to obtain gauge
- Cable needle
- Stitch holders

Gauge

10 sts and 13 rows = 4 inches/10cm in Cable & Rib pat
9 sts and 12 rows= 4 inches/10cm in Sleeve Rib pat
To save time, take time to check gauge.

Pattern Stitches
A. Cable & Rib

Row 1 (RS): K1, *p2, k4; rep from * to last 3 sts, p2, k1.
Rows 2 and 4: P1, *k2, p4; rep from * to last 3 sts, k2, p1.
Row 3: K1, *p2, k4, p2, place next 2 sts on cn and hold in front, k2, k2 from cn; rep from * to last 3 sts, p2, k1.
Rep Rows 1–4 for pat.

B. Sleeve Rib

Row 1: P2, *k4, p2; rep from * across.
Row 2: K2, *p4, k2; rep from * across.
Rep Rows 1–2 for pat.

Back

With CC cast on 46 (52, 58, 64, 70) sts.
Change to MC and p 1 row.
Work even in Cable & Rib pat until back measures 18 (18½, 18, 17, 18) inches, ending with a WS row.

Shape armhole

Next 2 rows: Bind off 2 (2, 3, 3, 3) sts, work in established pat to end of row. (42, 48, 52, 58 64 sts)
Row 3: Ssk, work in pat to last 2 sts, k2tog.
Row 4: Work even in pat.
Rep [Rows 3 and 4] 2 (5, 5, 6, 8) times more. (36, 36, 40, 42, 46 sts)
Work even until armhole measures 8½ (8½, 9¼, 10, 10) inches, ending with a WS row.

Shape shoulders

Bind off 5 (5, 5, 6, 6) sts at beg of next 2 rows,

then 6 (6, 6, 6, 7) sts at beg of following 2 rows. Place rem 14 (14, 18, 18, 20) sts on holder for back neck.

Front

Work as for back until armhole measures 6½ (6½, 6½, 7, 7) inches, ending with a WS row.

Shape neck

Work across 15 (15, 16, 17, 18) sts, place next 6 (6, 8, 8, 10) sts on holder for front neck, join 2nd ball of yarn and work across rem 15 (15, 16, 17, 18) sts.

Working on both sides of neck with separate balls of yarn, dec [1 st at each neck edge every row] 4 (4, 5, 5, 5) times. (11, 11, 11, 12, 13 sts) on each side.

Work even until armhole measures same as for back.

Shape shoulders

At each arm edge, bind off 5 (5, 5, 6, 6) sts once, then 6 (6, 6, 6, 7) sts once.

Sleeves

With CC, cast on 20 (22, 22, 24, 26) sts. Change to MC and purl 1 row.

Set up pat

Size extra-small and extra-large only (RS): [P2, k4] 3 (4) times, p2.

Size small and medium only (RS): K1 [p2, k4] 3 times, p2, k1.

Size large only (RS): K2 [p2, k4] 3 times, p2, k2.

Work in established Sleeve Rib pat, inc 1 st each end [every 6th row] 0 (0, 3, 3, 8) times, every 7th row 5 (3, 3, 4, 0) times, then every 8th row 1 (3, 0, 0, 0) times. (32, 34, 34, 38, 42 sts)

Work added sts into pat.

Work even until sleeve measures 16½ (17, 17, 17, 17¼) inches ending with a WS row.

Shape sleeve cap

Next 2 rows: Bind off 2 (2, 2, 2, 3) sts, work to end of row. (28, 30, 30, 34, 36 sts)

Dec 1 st each end [every row] 2 (3, 1, 2, 2) times, [every other row] 6 (5, 8, 8, 8) times, and finally [every row] 2 (3, 1, 2, 2) times.

Bind off rem 8 (8, 10, 10, 12) sts.

Collar

Sew left shoulder seam.

With RS facing using MC, knit across 14 (14, 18, 20, 20) sts of back neck holder, pick up and knit 11 (14, 14, 15, 15) sts along left neck edge, knit across 6 (6, 8, 8, 10) sts of front neck holder, pick up and knit 11 (14, 14, 16, 15) sts along right neck edge. (42, 48, 54, 60, 60 sts)

Note: Collar will fold over upon completion, therefore, WS of sweater will be facing you, but you will be working on RS of collar.

Next row: K2 [p2, k4] 6 (7, 8, 9, 9) times, p2, k2.

Work even in established Sleeve Rib pat until collar measures 5 (5, 5½, 5½, 6) inches, ending with a WS row.

Change to CC and bind off very loosely in pat.

Assembly

Sew rem shoulder seam and collar seam.
Sew sleeves into armholes, easing to fit.
Sew side and sleeve seams. ∎

Daisy Stitch Pullover

Design by Shari Haux

Daisies bloom on a field of soft yellow. A rolled collar adds a gentle touch.

Skill Level

INTERMEDIATE

Size
Woman's small (medium, large)
Instructions are given for smallest size, with larger sizes in parentheses. When only 1 number is given, it applies to all sizes.

Finished Measurements
Chest: 40 (44, 48) inches

Materials
- Brown Sheep Lamb's Pride Worsted 85 percent wool/15 percent mohair worsted weight yarn (190 yds/4 oz per skein): 7 (8, 8) skeins sun yellow #M13
- Size 6 (4mm) straight and 16-inch circular needles
- Size 8 (5mm) needles or size needed to obtain gauge
- Stitch holders
- Stitch markers

Gauge
18 sts and 24 rows = 4 inches/10cm in St st with larger needles
To save time, take time to check gauge.

Special Abbreviation
Daisy St: Insert RH needle in st 3 rows below 2nd st on LH needle and pull up a lp, [k2, pull a lp in same st as first lp] twice.

Pattern Stitches

A. Ridged Ribbing

Rows 1 and 3 (RS): P1, *k2, p1; rep from * across.

Row 2: K1, *p2, k1; rep from * across.

Row 4: Knit.

Rep Rows 1–4 for pat.

B. Daisy

Rows 1 (RS)–6: Work in St st.

Row 7: K8 (13, 7), Daisy st, *k6, Daisy st; rep from *, end last rep k8 (13, 7).

Row 8: P8 (13, 7), *p2tog, [p1, p2tog] twice, p5; rep from *, end last rep p7 (12, 6).

Row 9–14: Work in St st.

Row 15: K3 (8, 2), Daisy st, *k6, Daisy st; rep from *, end last rep k3 (8, 2).

Row 16: P3 (8, 2), *p2tog, [p1, p2tog] twice, p5; rep from *, end last rep p2 (7, 1).

Rep Rows 1–16 for pat.

Back

With smaller needles, cast on 79 (88, 97) sts.

Work even in Ridged Ribbing pat until back measures approx 2½ inches, ending with Row 2 of pat.

Change to larger needles and St st, inc 11 (12, 11) sts evenly on first row. (90, 100, 108 sts)

Work even until back measures 20½ (21½, 22½) inches, ending with a RS row.

Shape neck

P31 (35, 38) and sl to holder, bind off next 28 (30, 32) sts for back neck, p31 (35, 38) and sl to 2nd holder.

Front

Work ribbing as for back. Change to larger needles.

Begin Daisy pat, inc 11 (12, 11) sts evenly on first row. (90, 100, 108 sts)

Work even in Daisy pat until front measures 2½ (3, 3½) inches less than back, ending with a WS row.

Shape neck

Work in established pat across 38 (43, 47) sts, join 2nd ball of yarn and bind off 14 sts for front neck, work in pat to end of row.

Working on both sides of neck with separate balls of yarn, dec 1 st each side of neck [every other row] 7 (8, 9) times. (31, 35, 38 sts)

Work even until front measures same as back. Join front and back at shoulders using 3-needle bind-off method.

Neck Band

Beg at left shoulder with smaller circular needle and RS facing, pick up and knit 15 (15, 16) sts along left edge of neck, 14 sts of front neck, 15 (15, 16) sts along right neck edge, and 28 (30, 32) sts along back neck. 72 (74, 78) sts

Pm between first and last st.

Work even in k1, p1 ribbing for 1½ inch.

Change to St st and work even for ½ inch more. Bind off loosely.

Sleeves

Measure down 9 (10, 10½) inches from shoulder seam on front and back. Mark.

With RS facing, pick up and knit 74 (79, 82) sts between markers.

Work even in St st for 2 inches, ending with a WS row.

Dec 1 st each end on next and [every following 4th row] 14 (15, 15) times. (46, 49, 52 sts)

Work even until sleeve measures 15½ (16, 16½) inches, dec 6 sts evenly on last WS row. (40, 43, 46 sts)

Change to smaller needles.

Work even in Ridged Ribbing until cuff measures 2½ inches.

Bind off loosely.

Sew sleeve and side seams. ■

Purple Passion

Design by Sandi Prosser

A classically styled cabled pullover is a welcome addition to any winter wardrobe. Wear it for special occasions or just a walk in the woods.

Skill Level

INTERMEDIATE

Size

Woman's extra-small (small, medium, large)
Instructions are given for smallest size, with larger sizes in parentheses. When only 1 number is given, it applies to all sizes.

Finished Measurements

Chest: 34½ (37, 40½ , 43) inches
Length: 21 (21½ , 22, 22½) inches

Materials

- Brown Sheep Prairie Silks 72 percent wool/18 percent mohair/10 percent silk (88 yds/50g per ball): 14 (14, 15, 16) balls peseta purple #PS650
- Size 6 (4mm) needles
- Size 7 (4.5mm) needles or size needed to obtain gauge
- Cable needle
- Stitch markers
- Stitch holders

Gauge

20 sts and 26 rows = 4 inches/10cm in k2, p1 rib with larger needles
To save time, take time to check gauge.

Special Abbreviations

C5F (Cable 5 Front): Sl next 2 sts to cn and hold in front, k2, p1 from LH needle, k2 from cn.
C11F (Cable 11 Front): Sl next 5 sts to cn and hold in front, [k2, p1] twice, (k2, p1, k2) from cn.

Pattern Stitches

A. 2/1 Ribbing (multiple of 3 sts + 2)
Row 1 (RS): K2, *p1, k2; rep from * across.
Row 2: P2, *k1, p2; rep from * across.
Rep Rows 1 and 2 for pat.

B. Small Cable (panel of 13 sts)
Rows 1 and 3 (RS): P1, [k2, p1] 4 times.
Rows 2, 4 and 6: K1, [p2, k1] 4 times.
Row 5: P1, C5F, p1, C5F, p1.
Rep Rows 1–6 for pat.

C. Center Cable Panel (panel of 37 sts)
Row 1 and all RS rows except those listed below: P1, *k2, p1; rep from * across.
Row 2 and all WS rows: K1, *p2, k1; rep from * across.
Rows 11 and 21: P1, C11F, [p1, k2] 4 times, C11F, p1.
Row 31: P1, [k2, p1] 4 times, C11F, [p1, k2] 4 times, p1.
Row 42: Rep Row 2.
Rep Rows 3–42 for pat.

D. Sleeve Cable Panel (panel of 13 sts)
Row 1 and all RS rows except those listed below: P1, *k2, p1; rep from * across.
Row 2 and all WS rows: K1, *p2, k1; rep from * across.
Rows 11 and 21: P1, C11F, p1.
Row 42: Rep Row 2.
Rep Rows 3–42 for pat.

Back

With larger needles, cast on 86 (92, 101, 107) sts.
Work even in 2/1 Ribbing until back measures 3 inches, ending with a WS row.

Shape sides

Dec 1 st each end of next and [every following 4th row] 5 times. (74, 80, 89, 95 sts)

Work 5 rows even in 2/1 Ribbing.

Inc 1 st each end of next and [every following 4th row] 5 times, working incs into 2/1 Ribbing. (86, 92, 101, 107 sts)

Work even in established rib until back measures 13½ inches, ending with a WS row.

Shape armhole

Bind off 4 (4, 5, 6) sts beg next 2 rows.

Dec 1 st each end [every other row] 6 (7, 7, 8) times. (66, 70, 75, 79 sts)

Work even until armhole measures 7½ (8, 8½, 9) inches, ending with a WS row.

Shape shoulders

Bind off 5 (5, 6, 6) sts at beg of next 2 rows, then 5 (6, 6, 7) sts at beg of following 4 rows. Place rem 36 (36, 39, 39) sts on holder for back neck.

Front

Cast on 95 (101, 107, 113) sts.

Set up pat

Row 1 (RS): K2, [p1, k2] 9 (10, 11, 12) times, pm, work Row 1 of Small Cable, pm, [k2, p1] 3 times, k2, pm, work Row 1 of Small Cable, pm, k2, [p1, k2] 9 (10, 11, 12) times.

Row 2: P2, [k1, p2] 9 (10, 11, 12) times, work Row 2 of Small Cable, [p2, k1] 3 times, p2, work Row 2 of Small Cable, p2, [k1, p2] 9 (10, 11, 12) times.

Work even for 10 more rows as established. Remove markers.

Beg center panel

Row 1 (RS): K2, [p1, k2] 9 (10, 11, 12) times, pm, work Row 1 of Center Cable Panel, pm, k2, [p1, k2] 9 (10, 11, 12) times.

Row 2: P2, [k1, p2] 9 (10, 11, 12) times, work Row 2 of Center Cable Panel, p2, [k1, p2] 9 (10, 11, 12) times.

Work in established pat until front measures 13½ inches, *at the same time* shape sides as for back, ending with a WS row.

Shape armhole

Bind off 4 sts beg next 2 rows. (87, 93, 99, 105 sts)

Dec 1 st each end [every other row] 6 (7, 8, 8) times. (75, 79, 83, 89 sts)

Work even until armhole measures 5 (5½, 6, 6½) inches, ending with a WS row.

Shape shoulders & neck

Next row: Work across 25 (27, 28, 30) sts, place center 25 (25, 27, 29) sts on holder, join 2nd ball of yarn and work to end of row.

Working on both sides of neck with separate balls of yarn, bind off at each neck edge [3 sts] once, then [2 sts] once.

Dec 1 st each side of neck [every other row] 5 times. (15, 17, 18, 20 sts)
Work even until armhole measures same as for back.
Shape shoulders as for back.

Sleeves
Cast on 41 sts.
Set up pat
Row 1 (RS): K2, [p1, k2] 4 times, pm, work Row 1 of Small Cable, pm, k2, [p1, k2] 4 times.
Row 2: P2, [k1, p2] 4 times, work Row 2 of Small Cable, p2, [k1, p2] 4 times.
Work 10 more rows in established pat, inc 1 st each end of Row 7–43 sts.
Beg center panel
Row 1 (RS): [P1, k2] 5 times, work Row 1 of Sleeve Cable Panel, [k2, p1] 5 times.
Row 2: [K1, p2] 5 times, work Row 2 of Sleeve Cable Panel, [p2, k1] 5 times.
Continue in established pat inc 1 st each end [every 6th row] 10 (5, 12, 18) times, then [every 8th row] 2 (9, 4, 0) times. (67, 71, 75, 79 sts)
Work even until sleeve measures 19 inches, ending with a WS row.
Shape sleeve cap
Bind off 4 (4, 5, 6) sts at beg of next 2 rows.
Dec 1 st each end [every other row] 13 (15, 17, 18) times. (33, 33, 30, 31 sts)
Bind off 3 sts at beg of next 2 rows, then 4 sts at beg of following 2 rows.
Bind of rem 19 (19, 17, 17) sts.
Sew right shoulder seam.

Collar
With smaller needles and RS facing, pick up and knit 19 (19, 21, 20) sts along left neck edge, work in pat across 25 (25, 27, 29) sts of front neck, pick up and knit 19 (19, 21, 20) sts along right neck edge, work in pat across 36 (36, 39, 39) sts of back neck. (99, 99, 108, 108 sts)
Row 1 (WS): P1, *k1, p2; rep from * to last

2 sts, k1, p1.
Row 2: K1, *p1, k2; rep from * to last 2 sts, p1, k1.
Rep these 2 rows until collar measures 2 inches, inc 1 st at end of last WS row.
Pm at each end of last row.
Row 3: P1, *k2, p1; rep from * across.
Row 4: K1, *p2, k1; rep from * across
Rep rows 3 and 4 until collar measures 6½ inches.
Bind off in pat.

Assembly
Sew left shoulder and neck band seam, reversing seam at markers.
Sew in sleeves.
Sew side and sleeve seams. ∎

Intertwined Cables

Design by Melissa Leapman

A rugged, oversized pullover, suitable for either women or men, is perfect for chilly spring days.

Skill Level

■■■□
INTERMEDIATE

Size
Adult small (medium, large, extra-large)
Instructions are given for smallest size, with larger sizes in parentheses. When only 1 number is given, it applies to all sizes.

Finished Measurements
Chest: 40 (46½ , 53, 59) inches

Materials
• Brown Sheep Lamb's Pride Superwash Bulky 100 percent wool bulky weight yarn (110 yds/100g per skein): 14 (14, 16, 18) skeins serendipity turquoise #SW36
• Size 13 (9mm) needles or size needed to obtain gauge
• Cable needle
• Stitch markers
• ½-yd matching seam tape (optional)

Gauge
10 sts and 13 rows = 4 inches/10cm in St st with 2 strands of yarn held tog
To save time, take time to check gauge.

Special Abbreviations
C4R (Cable 4 Right): Sl 2 sts to cn and hold in back, k2, k2 from cn.
C4L (Cable 4 Left): Sl 2 sts to cn and hold in front, k2, k2 from cn.
T2R (Twist 2 Right): Sl 2 sts to cn and hold in back, k2, p1 from cn.
T2L (Twist 2 Left): Sl 2 sts to cn and hold in front, p1, k2 from cn.
M1 (Make 1): Make a backward lp and place on RH needle.

Pattern Stitches
A. 2/2 Rib
Row 1 (RS): K2, *p2, k2; rep from * across.
Row 2: P2, *k2, p2; rep from * across.
Rep Rows 1 and 2 for pat.
B. Cable Rib
Row 1 (RS): [P2, C4L] twice, p2.
Rows 2 and 4: [K2, p4] twice, k2.
Row 3: [P2, k4] twice, p2.
Rep Rows 1–4 for pat.
C. Cable Panel (panel of 14 sts)
Row 1 (RS): P1, [T2R, T2L] twice, p1.
Row 2 and all WS rows: Knit or purl the sts as they present themselves.
Rows 3 and 7: P1, k2, p2, C4R, p2, k2, p1.
Row 5: P1, k2, p2, k4, p2, k2, p1.
Row 9: P1, [T2L, T2R] twice, p1.
Row 11: P2, C4L, p2, C4R, p2.
Row 12: Rep Row 2.
Rep Rows 1–12 for pat.

Pattern Notes
Two strands of yarn are held tog for entire garment.
Instructions include one selvage st at each side; these sts are not reflected in final measurements.
Work fully fashioned sleeve inc on RS rows as follows: K2, M1, work to last 2 sts, M1, k2.

Back

With 2 strands of yarn held tog, cast on 58 (66, 74, 82) sts.

Set up pat (RS): Work 2/2 Rib over 22 (26, 30, 34) sts, pm, work Row 1 of Cable Rib over next 14 sts, pm, work 2/2 Rib to end of row.

Work even in established pats until ribbing measures approx 2½ inches, ending with Row 2 of Cable Rib.

Next row: Work in St st to marker, work Row 1 of Cable Panel over next 14 sts, work in St st to end.

Work even in newly established pats until back measures approx 16 inches, ending with a WS row.

Shape armholes

Bind off 8 (10, 12, 14) sts at beg of next 2 rows.

(42, 46, 50, 54 sts)

Work even until armhole measures 6 (7, 7, 8) inches, ending with a WS row.

Shape neck

Next row (RS): Work 10 (12, 14,16) sts, join 2nd ball of yarn and bind off next 22 sts, work to end of row.

Working on both sides of neck with separate balls of yarn, dec 1 st at each side of neck [every row] 6 times. (4, 6, 8, 10 sts)

Work even until armhole measures 9 (9½ , 9½, 10) inches.

Bind off.

Front

Work as for back until armhole measures 2½ (3, 3, 3½) inches, ending after Row 4 of Cable Panel.

Shape neck

Row 1 (RS): K14 (16, 18, 20) sts, k2tog, k1, p2, k2; join 2nd ball of yarn, k2, p2, k1, ssk, knit to end of row.

Row 2: Purl to within 7 sts of neck edge, p2tog-tbl, p1, k2, p2; with next ball of yarn p2, k2, p1, p2tog, purl to end row.

[Rep Rows 1 and 2] twice; rep Row 1 once. 14 (16, 18, 20) sts each side of neck.

Work Row 1 [every other row] 4 times. 10 (12, 14, 16) sts each side of neck.

Work even until armhole measures same as back to shoulders.

Shape shoulders

Bind off 4 (6, 8, 10) sts each shoulder edge once. 6 sts at each side of neck.

Back Neck Band

Work even on rem sts until bands, when slightly stretched, meet at center back neck.

Bind off.

Sleeves

With 2 strands of yarn held tog, cast on 26 sts.
Work even in 2/2 Rib until sleeve measures 2 inches, inc 1 st at end of last WS row. (27 sts)
Work in St st, making 1 fully fashioned inc at

each end [every other row] 0 (0, 0, 4) times,
[every 4th row] 3 (8, 11, 8) times, then [every
6th row] 7 (3, 0, 0) times. (47, 49, 49, 51 sts)
Work even until sleeve measures 21¾ (21½,
20¾, 19¾) inches.
Bind off.

Assembly

Sew shoulder seams.
Sew sides of neck band to back neck; sew
short ends of band tog at center back.
Sew sleeves into armholes.
Sew sleeve and side seams.
If desired, sew seam tape to inside of
shoulder and back neck seam to prevent
excess stretching. ■

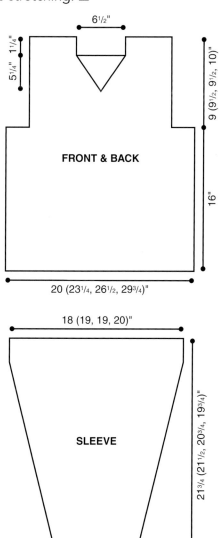

6½"

1¼"

5¼"

9 (9½, 9½, 10)"

FRONT & BACK

16"

20 (23¼, 26½, 29¾)"

18 (19, 19, 20)"

SLEEVE

21¾ (21½, 20¾, 19¾)"

10"

Autumn Harvest

Design by Sandi Prosser

A cable pattern gradually expands to form an attractive textured yoke and funnel collar on this fall-inspired pullover.

Skill Level

INTERMEDIATE

Size
Woman's small (medium, large, extra-large) Instructions are given for smallest size, with larger sizes in parentheses. When only 1 number is given, it applies to all sizes.

Finished Measurements
Chest: 39 (42½, 44, 46) inches
Length: 21 (21½, 22, 22½) inches

Materials
- Brown Sheep Lamb's Pride Worsted 85 percent wool/15 percent mohair worsted weight yarn (190 yds/4 oz per skein): 6 (7, 8, 9) skeins autumn harvest #M22
- Size 6 (4mm) needles
- Size 7 (4.5mm) needles or size needed to obtain gauge
- Cable needle
- Stitch markers

Gauge
19 sts and 26 rows = 4 inches/10cm in St st with larger needles
To save time, take time to check gauge.

Special Abbreviation
T2 (Twist 2): With needle in front of first st, knit 2nd st, then knit first st and sl both off needle.
C6F (Cable 6 Front): Sl next 3 sts to cn and hold in front, k3, k3 from cn.

M1 (Make 1): Pick up horizontal strand of yarn between stitch just worked and next st and knit it.

Pattern Stitch
Cable & Twisted Rib (multiple of 18 sts + 12)
Row 1 (RS): *P2, [T2, p1] twice, T2, p2, C6F; rep from *, end last rep p2.
Row 2 and all WS rows: Knit or purl the sts as they present themselves.
Rows 3, 5 and 7: *P2, [T2, p1] twice, T2, p2, k6; rep from *, end last rep p2.
Row 8: Rep Row 2.
Rep Rows 1–8 for pat.

Back
With smaller needles, cast on 93 (101, 105, 109) sts.
Beg with a knit row, work in St st for 7 rows.
Turning row (WS): Knit.
Change to larger needles.
Beg with a knit row, work even in St st until back measures 10½ (11, 11½ , 12) inches above turning row, ending with a WS row.
Beg pat
First inc row (RS): K37 (41, 43, 45), [M1, k2] twice, M1, k6, M1, k4, [M1, k2] twice, M1, k37 (41, 43, 45). 100 (108, 112, 116) sts
Row 2: P35 (39, 41, 43), pm, k2, p2, [k1, p2] twice, k2, p6, k2, p2, [k1, p2] twice, pm, k2, p35 (39, 41, 43).
Row 3: K35 (39, 41, 43), work Row 1 of Cable & Twisted Rib pat over next 30 sts, k35 (39, 41, 43).

Work even in established pat for 13 more rows.

2nd inc row (RS): K23 (27, 29, 31), [M1, k2] twice, k6, M1, k2, work Cable & Twisted Rib pat over next 30 sts, k3, M1, k4, [M1, k2] twice, M1, k23 (27, 29, 31). (108, 116, 120, 124 sts) Remove markers.

Row 2: P21 (25, 27, 29), pm, k2, p2, [k1, p2] twice, k2, p6, work Cable & Twisted Rib pat over next 30 sts, p6, k2, [p2, k1] twice, p2, k2, pm, p21 (25, 27, 29).

Row 3: K21 (25, 27, 29), work Cable & Twisted Rib pat over next 66 sts, k21 (25, 27, 29).

Work even in established pat for 13 more rows.

3rd inc row (RS): K9 (13, 15, 17), [M1, k2] twice, M1, k6, M1, k2, work Cable & Twisted Rib pat over next 66 sts, k3, M1, k4, M1, [k2, M1] twice, k9 (13, 15, 17). (116, 124, 128, 132 sts) Remove markers.

Row 2: P7 (11, 13, 15), pm, k2, p2, [k1, p2] twice, k2, p6, work Cable & Twisted Rib pat over next 66 sts, p6, k2, [p2, k1] twice, p2, k2, pm, p7 (11, 13, 15).

Row 3: K7 (11, 13, 15), work Cable & Twisted Rib pat over next 102 sts, k7 (11, 13, 15). Work even in established pat for 13 more rows.

Size small only:

4th inc row (RS): K5, M1, k2, work Cable & Twisted Rib pat as established, k2, M1, k5. (118 sts)

Row 2: K2, p6, work Cable & Twisted Rib pat as established, p6, k2.

Row 3: P2, C6F, work Cable & Twisted Rib pattern, C6F, p2.

Work even in established pat until back measures 20 inches above turning row, ending with a WS row.

Size medium, large and extra-large only:

4th inc row (RS): K1, [M1, k2] 1 (2, 3) times, M1, k6, M1, k2 work Cable & Twisted Rib pat as established, k2, M1, k6, [M1, k2] 1 (2, 3) times, M1, k1. (130, 136, 142 sts)

Row 2: [K1, p2] 2 (3, 4) times, k2, p6, work Cable & Twisted Rib pat as established, p6, k2, [p2, k1] 2 (3, 4) times.

Row 3: [P1, T2] 2 (3, 4) times, p2, C6F, work Cable & Twisted Rib pat as established, C6F, p2, [T2, p1] 2 (3, 4) times.

Work even in established pat until back measures 20½ (21, 21½) inches above turning row, ending with a WS row.

All sizes:

Shape shoulders

Working k2tog over each T2 and dec 1 st over each cable, bind off 9 (9, 10, 11) sts at beg of next 4 rows, then 8 (10, 10, 10) sts at beg of following 2 rows. (56 sts)

Collar

Work even in established pat for 2½ inches more, ending with a WS row.

Next row: Knit, working k2tog over each T2 and dec 1 st over cable.

Bind off all sts knitwise.

Front

Work as for back.

Sleeves

With smaller needles, cast on 46 (48, 50, 52) sts

Beg with a knit row, work in St st for 7 rows.

Turning row (WS): Knit.

Change to larger needles.

Beg with a knit row, work in St st for 9 rows.

Inc 1 st each end of next and [every following 4th row] 11 (11, 13, 14) times, then [every 6th row] 9 (10, 10, 10) times. (86, 90, 96, 100 sts)

Work even until sleeve measures 18 (18, 18½, 19) inches above turning row.

Bind off.

Assembly

Sew shoulder and neck seams.

Measure down 9 (9½, 10, 10½) inches from shoulder seam on front and back. Mark for underarm.

Sew sleeves to body between markers.

Sew sleeve and side seams.

Turn body and sleeve facings to inside and sew loosely in place. ▓

Purple Pop Over

Design by Barbara Venishnick

At the end of a busy day, pull on a pair of leggings, "pop" on a roomy, comfortable top, and relax.

Skill Level
■■□□
EASY

Size
Woman's small (medium, large) Instructions are given for smallest size, with larger sizes in parentheses. When only 1 number is given, it applies to all sizes.

Finished Measurements
Chest: 44 (48, 52) inches
Length: 23 (24, 25) inches

Materials
- Brown Sheep Lamb's Pride Worsted 85 percent wool/15 percent mohair worsted weight yarn (190 yds/4 oz per skein): 10 (10, 11) skeins supreme purple #M100
- Size 13 (9mm) straight and 16-inch circular needles or size needed to obtain gauge
- Stitch holders
- Stitch markers

Gauge
10½ sts and 19 rows = 4 inches/10cm in garter st with 2 strands of yarn held tog
To save time, take time to check gauge.

Pattern Notes
Sl last st of every row with yarn in front.
Entire garment is worked holding 2 strands of yarn tog.

Back
Cast on 59 (65, 71) sts.
Work even in garter st until back measures 20 (21, 22) inches, ending with a WS row.
Shape shoulders
Bind off 4 (4, 5) sts at the beg of next 4 rows, 3 (4, 4) sts at the beg of following 6 rows, and finally 3 (3, 4) sts at beg of next 2 rows.
Place rem 19 sts on holder for back neck.

Front
Work as for back until front measures 20 (21, 22) inches, ending with a WS row.
Shape front neck and shoulders
Place center 13 sts on holder.
Working on both sides of neck with separate balls of yarn, dec [1 st each side of neck every RS row] 3 times, *at the same time,* shape shoulders as for back.

Sleeves
Cast on 32 sts.
Work even in rev St st for 3 inches, ending with a WS row.
Work in garter st for 14 rows (7 ridges).
Inc row (RS): K1-tbl, knit into front and back of next st, knit to last 2 sts, knit into front and back of next st, sl 1 wyif.
Knit 5 rows.
[Rep last 6 rows] 7 times more. (48 sts)
Knit 3 rows.
Shape sleeve cap
Bind off 2 sts at beg of next 6 rows, then 3 sts at beg of following 8 rows.
Bind off rem 12 sts.

k 7 sts along left edge of neck. (46 sts)
Pm between first and last st.
Purl 1 rnd, [k 1 rnd, p 1 rnd] 3 times.
Knit 4 rounds for facing.
Bind off all sts loosely.
Fold facing to inside and sew in place.

Finishing

Measure 10 inches down from shoulder seam
on front and back and mark for armhole.
Sew sleeves into armhole between markers.
Fold sleeve inside out and sew St st section tog,
turn sleeve to RS and complete seam.
Sew side seams.
Referring to schematic, sew pockets to front
of sweater. ∎

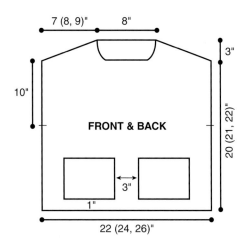

Pockets

Make 2

Cast on 18 sts.
Work even in St st until pocket measures
6 inches, ending with a RS row.
Bind off knitwise on WS of work.
Sew shoulder seams.

Neck Band

With circular needle and RS of work facing, knit
across 19 sts from back neck holder, pick up and
k 7 sts along right edge of neck, knit across 13
sts from front neck holder, pick up and

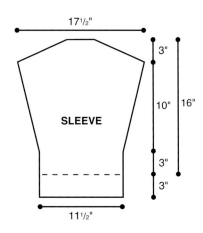

Monterey Bay

Design by Diane Zangl

Texture-on-texture provides an interesting approach to this man's pullover. Columns of cables hopscotch over bands of Quaker Rib. The cable motif is repeated in a ribbed version for the cuffs and bands.

Skill Level

INTERMEDIATE

Size

Man's small (medium, large, extra-large) Instructions are given for smallest size, with larger sizes in parentheses. When only 1 number is given, it applies to all sizes. Model shown in size medium.

Finished Measurements

Chest: 43 (45, 48, 50) inches
Armhole depth: 9 (9½, 10, 11) inches
Side to underarm: 17 (18, 19, 19) inches
Sleeve length: 18 (19, 20, 21) inches

Materials

- Brown Sheep Lamb's Pride Worsted 85 percent wool/15 percent mohair worsted weight yarn (190 yds/4 oz per skein): 7 (8, 9, 10) skeins prairie fire #M181
- Size 6 (4mm) straight and 16-inch circular needles
- Size 7 (4.5mm) needles or size needed to obtain gauge
- Stitch markers
- Stitch holder

Gauge

16 sts and 24 rows = 4 inches/10cm in St st with larger needles

17 sts and 26 rows = 4 inches/10cm in pat st with larger needles
To save time, take time to check gauge.

Special Terms

Single Twist: K2tog leaving sts on needle, insert RH needle between sts and knit first st again, sl both sts off needle.

Double Twist: With needle behind work, knit in back lp of 2nd st, knit in front of first st, sl both sts off needle; k2tog leaving sts on needle, insert RH needle between sts and knit first st again, sl both sts off needle.

Pattern Notes

For ease in working, pm on each side of cable columns.

Depending on chosen size, the position of lowest cable columns on body and sleeves may need to be adjusted to align with ribbing pat. If a cable column falls near a seam line, move it inward or do not work it—knitter's choice.

Cable columns should be worked at least 2 sts away from edge for ease of seaming.

When working neck band, read all rows of Chart A from right to left. Work 5-st rep only.

Back

With smaller needles, cast on 91 (96, 101, 106) sts. Referring to Chart A, work even in Twisted Cable pat for 12 rows, changing to larger needles and inc 1 (0, 1, 0) sts on last row. (92, 96, 102, 106 sts)

Referring to Chart B for cable column placement, work even in pat until back measures 17 (18, 19, 19) inches, ending with a WS row.

Shape underarm

Rows 1 and 2: Bind off 8 (8, 9, 10) sts, work in pat to end of row.

Row 3: K1, ssk, work in pat to last 3 sts, k2tog, k1.

Row 4: P2, work in pat to last 2 sts, p2.

Rep [Rows 3 and 4] 3 (3, 3, 4) times more. (68, 72, 76, 76 sts)

Work even until armhole measures 9 (9½, 10, 11) inches.

Bind off all sts. Mark center 30 (32, 34, 34) sts for back neck.

Front

Work as for back until armhole measures 5½ (6, 6, 7) inches, ending with a WS row.

Shape neck

Place center 18 (20, 22, 22) sts on holder. Working on both sides of neck with separate balls of yarn, dec 1 st at each side of neck [every other row] 6 times as follows:

RS rows: Work in pat to last 3 sts of left front,

k2tog, k1; with 2nd ball of yarn k1, ssk, work in pat to end of row.

WS rows: Work in pat to last 2 sts, p2; with 2nd ball of yarn p2, work in pat to end of row.

Work even on rem 19 (20, 21, 21) sts at each side of neck until armhole measures same as for back.

Bind off all sts.

Sew shoulder seams.

Neck band

With smaller circular needles, pick up and knit 30 sts along back neck, 21 (20, 25, 25) sts along left edge, knit across front neck, dec 2 sts on sizes large and extra-large only, pick up and knit 21 (20, 25, 25) sts along right edge. (90, 90, 100, 100 sts)

Pm between first and last st.

Rnd 1: *P1, k4; rep from * around.

Work even in Twisted Cable pat for 8 rnds. Bind off loosely in pat.

Sleeves

With smaller needles, cast on 31 (36, 36, 41) sts. Referring to Chart A, work even in Twisted Cable pat for 16 rows, inc 3 (0, 2, 1) sts on last row. (34, 36, 38, 42 sts)

Referring to Chart C for cable column placement, inc 1 st at each end [every 4th row] 21 (22, 24, 26) times. (76, 80, 86, 94 sts)

Work even until sleeve measures 18 (19, 20, 21) inches, ending with a WS row. Mark each end st for underarm.

Shape sleeve cap

Work even for 10 (10, 12, 12) more rows.
Next row (RS): K1, ssk, work in pat to last 3 sts, k2tog, k1.

CHART A
Twisted Cable

STITCH KEY
☐ K on RS, p on WS
☐ P on RS, k on WS
☐ Single twist
☐ Double twist

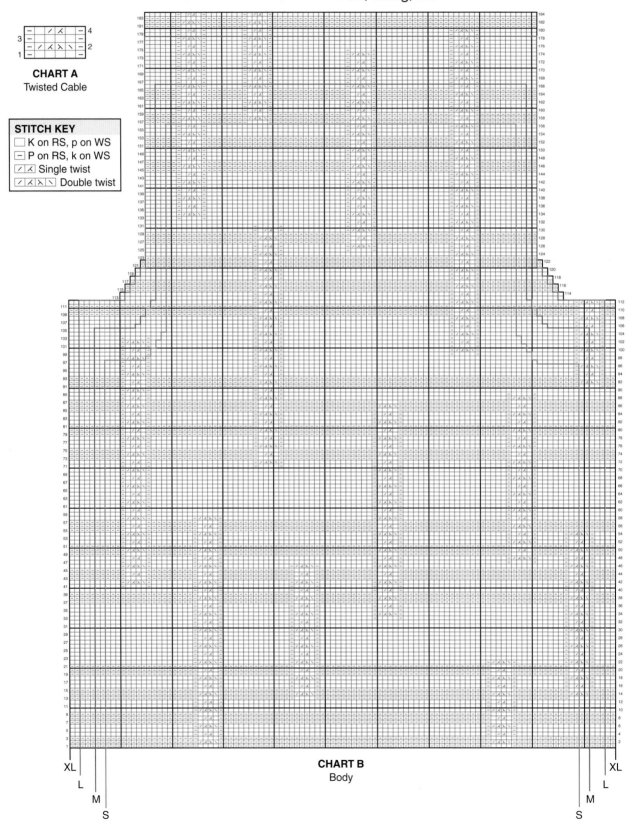

CHART B
Body

Row 2: P2, work in pat to last 2 sts, p2.
Rep last 2 rows 3 (3, 3, 4) times more.
Bind off rem 68 (72, 78, 84) sts.

Assembly

Sew sleeves into armholes, matching underarm markers to first bound-off underarm st of body. Sew sleeve and side seams. ■

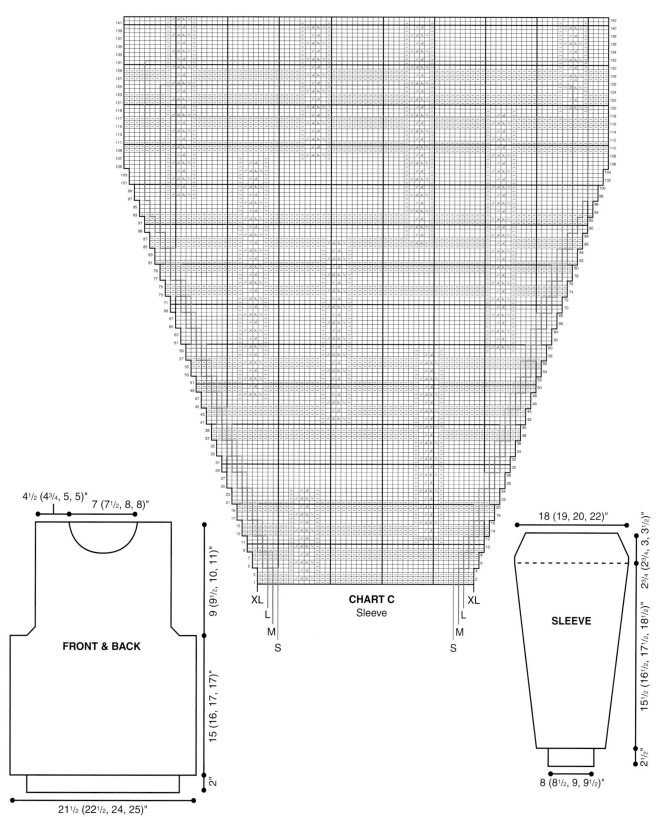

CHART C
Sleeve

FRONT & BACK

4½ (4¾, 5, 5)"
7 (7½, 8, 8)"
9 (9½, 10, 11)"
15 (16, 17, 17)"
2"
21½ (22½, 24, 25)"

SLEEVE

18 (19, 20, 22)"
2¾ (2¾, 3, 3½)"
15½ (16½, 17½, 18½)"
2½"
8 (8½, 9, 9½)"

Dappled Forest Glen

Design by Melissa Leapman

Flared sleeves add a unique touch to a basic pullover.

Skill Level

EASY

Size

Woman's small (medium, large, extra-large, 2X-large) Instructions are given for smallest size, with larger sizes in parentheses. When only 1 number is given, it applies to all sizes.

Finished Measurements

Chest: 37 (40, 43½, 47, 51) inches

Materials

- Brown Sheep Handpaint Originals 70 percent mohair/30 percent wool worsted weight yarn (88 yds/50g per hank): 11 (12, 13, 14, 15) hanks forest floor #HP70

4 MEDIUM

- Size 8 (5mm) needles or size needed to obtain gauge

Gauge

18 sts and 24 rows = 4 inches/10cm in St st
To save time, take time to check gauge.

Special Abbreviation

M1 (Make 1): Make a backwards lp and place on RH needle.

Pattern Notes

In order to distribute color randomly, work two-row stripes, alternating from two different balls of yarn, and carrying yarn up side of work.
For fully fashioned dec, work as follows:
On RS rows: K3, ssk, work to last 5 sts, k2tog, k3.

On WS rows: P3, p2tog, work to last 5 sts, p2tog-tbl, p3.
For fully fashioned inc, work as follows:
On RS rows: K2, M1, work to last 2 sts, M1, k2.

Back

Cast on 75 (81, 88, 95, 102) sts. Work even in garter St for 1 inch, inc 9 (9, 10, 11, 12) sts evenly on last WS row. (84, 90, 98, 106, 114 sts)
Change to St st and work even until back measures 14 (14½, 14½, 15, 15) inches, ending with a WS row.

Shape armholes

Next 2 rows: Bind off 2 (3, 4, 6, 6) sts, work to end of row. (80, 84, 90, 94, 104 sts)
Work fully fashioned dec at each end [every row] 4 (5, 9, 9, 14) times, then [every other row] 6 (7, 5, 6, 4) times. (60, 62, 64, 64, 66 sts)
Work even until armhole measures 7 (7½, 7½, 8, 8½) inches, ending with a WS row.

Shape shoulders

Bind off 4 (4, 5, 5, 5) sts at beg of next 4 rows, then 5 (5, 4, 5, 6) sts at beg of following 2 rows.
Bind off rem 34 sts.

Front

Work as for back until armhole measures 4½ (5, 5, 5½, 6) inches, ending with a WS row.

Shape neck

Next row (RS): K 22 (22, 23, 24, 25) sts, join 2nd ball of yarn and bind off next 16 sts for front neck, knit to end of row.
Working on both sides of neck with separate balls of yarn, bind off at each neck edge [2 sts] twice.

Dec 1 st each side of neck [every row] twice, then [every other row] 3 times. 13 (13, 14, 15, 16) sts Work even until armhole measures same as for back.

Shape shoulders

At each arm edge, bind off 4 (4, 5, 5, 5) sts twice, then 5 (5, 4, 5, 6) sts once.

Sleeves

Cast on 53 (55, 55, 56, 56) sts. Work even in garter St for 1 inch, inc 6 (6, 6, 7, 7) sts evenly on last WS row. (59, 61, 61, 63, 63 sts) Change to St st.

Shape sleeve flare

Work fully fashioned dec at each end [every 4th row] 9 times. (41, 43, 43, 45, 45 sts) Work even until sleeve measures 9 (9, 9, 9½, 9½) inches, ending with a WS row.

Begin sleeve shaping

Work fully fashioned inc at each end [every 4th row] 0 (0, 0, 0, 3) times, [every 6th row] 6 (4, 4, 8, 6) times, and finally [every 8th row] 1 (3, 3, 0, 0) times. (55, 57, 57, 61, 63 sts) Work even until sleeve measures 17½ (18, 18½, 19, 19) inches, ending with a WS row.

Shape sleeve cap

Next 2 rows: Bind off 2 (3, 4, 6, 6) sts, work to end of row. (51, 51, 49, 49, 51 sts) Work fully fashioned dec at each end [every other row] 6 (9, 10, 13, 15) times, then [every row] 11 (8, 6, 3, 2) times. (17 sts) Bind off 2 sts at beg of next 4 rows. Bind off rem 9 sts. Sew left shoulder seam.

Neck Band

With RS facing, pick up and k 84 sts around neckline. Work even in garter st for ½ inch, ending with a WS row. **Next row (RS):** Knit, dec 12 sts evenly. (72 sts) Work even in garter st until neck band measures 1 inch, ending with a WS row. Bind off loosely.

Assembly

Sew right shoulder seam, including side of neck band. Sew in sleeves. Sew sleeve and side seams. ∎

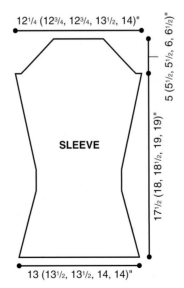

12¼ (12¾, 12¾, 13½, 14)"

5 (5½, 5½, 6, 6½)"

17½ (18, 18½, 19, 19)"

SLEEVE

13 (13½, 13½, 14, 14)"

7½"

3½"

1"

7 (7½, 7½, 8, 8½)"

FRONT & BACK

14 (14½, 14½, 15, 15½)"

18½ (20, 21¾, 23½, 25½)"

Checks & Stripes Twin Set

Designs by Kennita Tully

Take a colorful tank top, add a vivid cardigan, and your wardrobe possibilities become greatly expanded.

Skill Level

EASY

Size
Woman's small (medium, large, extra-large) Instructions are given for smallest size, with larger sizes in parentheses. When only 1 number is given, it applies to all sizes.

Finished Measurements
Tank
Chest: 36 (39½, 42, 45) inches
Length: 19 (20, 21, 22) inches
Cardigan
Chest: 38 (42, 46, 50) inches
Length: 20 (21, 22, 23) inches

Materials
Tank
- Brown Sheep Cotton Fleece 80 percent Pima cotton/20 percent Merino wool worsted weight yarn (215 yds/100g per skein): 3 (3, 4, 4) skeins tea rose #CW210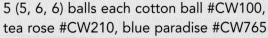
- Size 5 (3.75mm) 16-inch circular needle
- Size 6 (4mm) needles or size needed to obtain gauge
- Stitch markers
Cardigan
- Brown Sheep Cotton Fine 80 percent Pima cotton/20 percent Merino wool fingering weight yarn (222 yds/50g per ball):

5 (5, 6, 6) balls each cotton ball #CW100, tea rose #CW210, blue paradise #CW765
- Size 6 (4mm) needles
- Size 8 (5mm) needles or size needed to obtain gauge
- Stitch markers
- 1 (1-inch) button

Gauge
Tank
18 sts and 28 rows = 4 inches/10cm in Wide Shadow Rib pat with larger needles
Cardigan
18 sts and 28 rows = 4 inches/10cm in Slip Stitch Mesh pat with larger needles
To save time, take time to check gauge.

Pattern Stitches
A. Narrow Shadow Rib (multiple of 3 sts + 2)
Row 1 (RS): P2, *k1-tbl, p2; rep from * across.
Row 2: Knit.
Rep Rows 1 and 2 for pat.
B. Wide Shadow Rib (multiple of 6 sts + 5)
Row 1 (RS): P5, *k1-tbl, p5; rep from * across.
Row 2: Knit.
Rep Rows 1 and 2 for pat.
C. Twisted Rib (multiple of 3 sts)
All rnds: *K1-tbl, p2; rep from * around.
D. Slip Stitch Mesh
Row 1 (RS): Purl.
Row 2: Knit.
Row 3: K2, *sl 1 wyib, k1; rep from * to last

2 sts, k2.

Row 4: K2, *sl 1 wyif, k1; rep from * to last
2 sts, k2.

Row 5: K2, *yo, k2tog; rep from * to last
2 sts, k2.

Row 6: Purl.

Rep Rows 1–6 for pat.

Pattern Note

Hold 1 strand of each color tog for entire
cardigan.

Shadow Rib Tank

Back

With larger needles, cast on 83 (89, 95, 101) sts.
Work even in Narrow Shadow Rib for 4 rows.
Change to Wide Shadow Rib and work even
until back measures 12 (12½, 13, 13½) inches,
ending with a WS row.

Shape armholes

Next 2 rows: Bind off 6 (7, 7, 7) sts, work to
end of row. (71, 75, 81, 87 sts)

Dec row: Ssk, work in pat to last 2 sts, k2tog.
Work dec row [every other row] 4 (4, 5, 5) times,
then [every 4th row] twice. (59, 63, 67, 73 sts)
Work even until armhole measures 7 (7½, 8, 8½)
inches, ending with a WS row.

Shape shoulders and neck

Next row (RS): Bind off 6 (5, 6, 7) sts, work
across next 10 (12, 12, 12) sts, k2tog, place
rem sts on holder.

[Bind off 5 (6, 6, 6) sts at arm edge] twice.
Sl sts from holder to needle. With RS facing,
join yarn at next st.

Bind off 25 (27, 29, 33) sts, ssk, work to end
of row.

Bind off at arm edge 6 (5, 6, 7) sts once, then
5 (6, 6, 6) sts twice.

Front

Work as for back until armhole measures 4 (4½,
5, 5½) inches, ending with a WS row.

Shape neck

Work across 22 (23, 24, 26) sts, attach 2nd ball

of yam. Bind off next 15 (17, 19, 21) sts for front
neck, work to end of row.

Working on both sides of neck with separate
balls of yarn, bind off 2 sts at each neck edge.
Dec 1 st at each neck edge [every other row]
2 (2, 2, 3) times, then [every 4th row] twice.
(16, 17, 18, 19 sts)

Work even until armhole measures same
as back.

Shape shoulders

Bind off at each arm edge 6 (5, 6, 7) sts once,
then 5 (6, 6, 6) sts twice.

Sew shoulder and side seams.

Armbands

Beg at underarm with smaller circular needle,
pick up and k 90 (93, 99, 102) sts around
armhole. Join, pm between first and last st.
Work in Twisted Rib pat for 2 rnds.

Bind off in pat.

Neck Band

Beg at right shoulder with smaller circular needle, pick up and knit 33 (34, 38, 41) sts along back neck to left shoulder, 18 (18, 18, 20) sts along left side neck, 15 (17, 19, 21) sts along front neck and 18 (18, 18, 20) sts along right side of neck. (84, 87, 93, 102 sts)
Work in Twisted Rib pat for 2 rnds.
Bind off in pat.

Slip Stitch Mesh Cardigan

Back

With larger needles, cast on 86 (94, 106, 114) sts.
Work even in Slip Stitch Mesh pat until back measures 12 (12½, 13, 13½) inches.
Mark each end st of last row for underarm.
Work even until back measures approx 20 (21, 22, 23) inches, ending with Row 2 of pat.
Bind off.

Front

(make both alike)
With larger needles, cast on 42 (46, 52, 56) sts.
Work as for back.

Sleeves

With larger needles, cast on 36 (40, 44, 48) sts.
Working in Slip Stitch Mesh pat, inc 1 st each end [every 6th row] 3 times, then [every 8th row] 14 times. (72, 76, 80, 84 sts)
Work even until sleeve measures approx 20 inches, ending with Row 2 of pat.
Bind off.

Assembly

Pm for shoulder 6 (6½, 7½, 8½) inches from armhole on all pieces.
Sew shoulder seams.
Sew sleeves to body between underarm markers.
Sew sleeve and side seams.

Button Band

Beg at top edge with smaller needles and RS facing, pick up and purl [2 sts for every 3 rows] 12 (12, 14, 14) times, pm, then pick up and knit at the same ratio to lower edge. Record number of picked-up sts after marker.
Knit 4 rows.
Bind off.
Mark top 24 (24, 28, 28) sts for collar.

Buttonhole Band

Beg at lower edge with smaller needles and RS facing, working at a 2:3 ratio as before, pick up and knit recorded number of sts for button band, pm, pick up and purl 24 (24, 28, 28) sts to top edge.
Knit 1 row.
Buttonhole row: Knit to 4 sts before marker, bind off next 4 sts, knit to end of row.

Knit 2 more rows, casting on 4 sts over previous bound-off area.
Bind off.
Mark top 24 (24, 28, 28) sts for collar.

Collar Edging

With WS facing, pick up and knit 18 (19, 21, 21) sts across left front to shoulder, pick up and purl 33 (35, 37, 37) sts across back neck, pick up and knit 18 (19, 21, 21) sts across right front. (69, 73, 79, 79 sts)
Knit 4 rows.
Bind off.

Turn collar back at marked st. Tack collar point to front of cardigan.
Sew on button. ▥

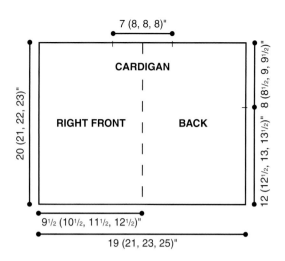

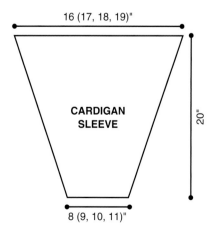

Lovely Lace Turtleneck

Design by Colleen Smitherman

The lovely lace borders, which work up swiftly on this sweater, have their roots in the Feather and Fan pattern from the Shetland Islands.

Skill Level

INTERMEDIATE

Size

Woman's small (medium, large, extra-large) Instructions are given for smallest size, with larger sizes in parentheses. When only 1 number is given, it applies to all sizes.

Finished Measurements

Chest: 36 (40, 44, 48) inches
Length: 18½ (19½, 20½, 21) inches

Materials

- Brown Sheep Cotton Fleece 80 percent Pima cotton/20 percent Merino wool worsted weight yarn (215 yds/100g per skein): 4 (5, 5, 6) skeins putty #CW105
- Size 6 (4mm) needles or size needed to obtain gauge
- Size 7 (4.5mm) needles
- Stitch holders

Gauge

20 sts and 28 rows = 4 inches/10cm in St st with smaller needles
To save time, take time to check gauge.

Special Abbreviation

Wrap: Work to turning point, sl next st purlwise wyif, take yarn to WS, return st to LH needle, turn. When working wrap and st tog, lift st onto needle so it will be on WS, then knit or purl st and wrap tog.

Back

With smaller needles, cast on 90 (101, 112, 123) sts.
Knit 5 rows.
Set up pat (RS): K1, [work Row 1 of Lace Chart] 8 (9, 10, 11) times, k1.
Keeping first and last st in St st for selvage, work even in established pat until 17 rows of chart are complete.
Work even in St st until back measures 10 (10½, 10½, 10½) inches, ending with a WS row.

Shape armholes

Bind off 4 (4, 7, 10) sts at beg of next 2 rows. (82, 93, 98, 103 sts)
Dec 1 st each end [every other row] 7 (10, 12, 13) times. (68, 73, 74, 77 sts)
Work even until armhole measures 6½ (7, 7½, 8) inches, ending with a WS row.

Shape neck

K25 (30, 26, 31), join 2nd ball of yarn and bind off next 18 (13, 22, 15) sts, knit to end of row.
Working on both sides of neck with separate balls of yarn, bind off at each neck edge 4 (6, 4, 6) sts once, 1 (3, 1, 2) sts 3 (1, 2, 1) times, and 0 (1, 0, 1) sts 0 (2, 0, 2) times. (18, 19, 20, 21 sts)
At the same time, shape shoulders as follows:
Row 1 (RS): Work across right shoulder, work across left shoulder to last 3 (4, 5, 5) sts, wrap next st and turn.
Row 2: Work across left shoulder, work across right shoulder to last 3 (4, 5, 5) sts, wrap next st and turn.
Rows 3 and 5: Work across right shoulder, work across left shoulder to 5 sts before last wrapped st, wrap next st and turn.

Rows 4 and 6: Work across left shoulder, work across right shoulder to 5 sts before last wrapped st, wrap next st and turn.

Row 7: Work across right shoulder to neck edge, work across all left shoulder sts, working wraps and sts tog as you come to them.

Row 8: Work across 18 (19, 20, 21) left shoulder sts, work across all right shoulder sts, working wraps and sts tog as you come to them. Place shoulder sts on holders.

Front

Work as for back until armhole measures 5¼ (5½, 6, 6¾) inches, ending with a WS row.

Shape neck

K29 (35, 33, 37), join 2nd ball of yarn and bind off next 10 (3, 8, 3) sts, knit to end of row. Working both sides of neck with separate balls of yarn, bind off at each neck edge 2 (6, 4, 6) sts once, 1 (2, 2, 2) sts 9 (1, 1, 2) times, and 0 (1, 1, 1) sts 0 (8, 7, 6) times. (18, 19, 20, 21 sts)

At the same time, shape shoulders as for back.

Sleeves

With smaller needles, cast on 37 (46, 46, 48) sts. Knit 5 rows.

Set up pat (RS): K2 (1, 1, 2), pm, [work Row 1 of Lace Chart] 3 (4, 4, 4) times, pm, k2 (1, 1, 2). Keeping first and last 2 (1, 1, 2) sts in St st, work even in established pat until Row 17 of chart is complete.

Working in St st, inc 1 st each end [every 6th (8th, 6th, 6th) row] 2 (7, 7, 18) times, then [every 8th (9th, 8th, 0) rows] 13 (6, 9, 0) times. (67, 72, 78, 84 sts)

Work even until sleeve measures 16 (16¼, 15¾, 15½) inches, ending with a WS row.

Shape sleeve cap

Bind off 5 (5, 4, 4) sts at beg of next 2 (2, 4, 4) rows. (57, 62, 62, 68 sts)

Dec 1 st each end [every row] 5 (7, 3, 7) times, [every 3rd row] 0 (0, 0, 10) times, then [every other row] 15 (15, 18, 7) times. (17, 18, 20, 20 sts)

Sizes large and extra-large only: Bind off 3 (4)

sts at beg of next 2 rows.
Bind off rem 17 (18, 14, 12) sts.

Turtleneck Collar

With larger needles, cast on 90 sts.
Knit 5 rows.
Set up pat (RS): K1, [work Row 1 of
Lace Chart] 8 times, k1.
Keeping first and last st in St st for sel-
vage, work even in established pat until
Row 5 of chart is complete.
Work even in St st until collar measures
5 inches.
Change to smaller needles and work
even for 1 inch more.
Bind off loosely.

Assembly

Join shoulders using 3-needle bind-off
method.
Sew short ends of collar tog.
Having seam at center back and
centering scallop at front, sew collar to
neck opening, making sure sts are loose
enough for turtleneck to fit over head.
Sew sleeves into armholes.
Sew side and sleeve seams. ■

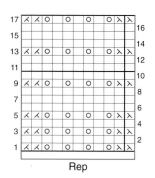

Rep

LACE CHART

STITCH KEY
☐ K on RS, p on WS
⟍ Ssk
○ Yo
⟋ K2tog

My Dog & Me

Designs by Bonnie Franz

For your morning walk, dress your dog in style with a sweater to match your pullover.

Skill Level

EASY

Size

Adult extra-small (small, medium, large, extra-large, 2X-large) Dog sweater is one size. Instructions are given for smallest size, with larger sizes in parentheses. When only 1 number is given, it applies to all sizes.

Finished Measurements

Pullover
Chest: 32 (36½, 40, 43½, 48, 51½) inches
Length: 23 (24, 25, 26½, 27½, 28½) inches
Sleeve length: 16½ (17½, 17½, 18, 18½, 19½) inches
Dog Sweater
Around stomach: 17½ inches
Length: 14 inches

Materials

- Brown Sheep Lamb's Pride Superwash Bulky 100 percent wool bulky weight yarn (110 yds/100g per skein): 7 (7, 8, 9, 10, 11) amethyst #SW62 (MC), 2 (2, 3, 3, 4, 4) skeins blaze #SW145 (CC)
- Size 9 (5.5mm) 16-inch circular and double-pointed needles
- Size 10½ (6.5mm) 16-, 24- and 36-inch circular and double-pointed needles or size needed to obtain gauge
- Stitch markers
- Stitch holders
- 1 toggle button

Blocked Gauge

14 sts and 21 rows = 4 inches/10cm in St st with larger needles
To save time, take time to check gauge.

Stripe Sequence

Work in St st for 6 rnds/rows MC, 1 rnd each CC, MC, CC.
Rep these 9 rnds for pat.

Pattern Notes

Pullover is worked in the round on circular needles to the underarm.
Upper portion is worked back and forth in rows. Sleeves are worked on double-pointed and circular needles in the round.
Dog sweater may be made larger by adding 4 sts for every added 1 inch of body girth. Add extra length after body band.

Pullover

Body

With MC and smaller needles, cast on 50 (58, 62, 68, 76, 80) sts, pm, cast on 50 (58, 62, 68, 76, 80) sts.
Join without twisting, pm between first and last st.
Work in k1, p1 ribbing for 2 inches, inc 12 (12, 16, 16, 16, 20) sts evenly on last rnd. (112, 128, 140, 152, 168, 180 sts)
Change to larger needles.
Work even in Stripe Sequence until body measures 14 (14½, 15, 15½, 16, 16) inches.

Divide for front and back
K 56 (64, 70, 76, 84, 90) sts and place on holder for front, knit to end of row.

Back
Work in rows from this point in established color sequence until armhole measures 9 (9½, 10, 11, 11½, 12½) inches.
Bind off all sts.

Front
Sl sts from holder to needle.

Work as for back until armhole measures 6 (6½, 7, 8, 8, 9) inches, ending with a WS row.
Shape neck
Next row: K 22 (25, 28, 30, 34, 37) sts, place center 12 (14, 14, 16, 16, 16) sts on holder, join 2nd ball of yarn and k 22 (25, 28, 30, 34, 37) sts. Working on both sides of neck with separate balls of yarn, dec 1 st at each neck edge [every other row] 4 (4, 5, 5, 5, 6) times. (18, 21, 23, 25, 29, 31 sts)
Work even until armhole measures same as for back.
Bind off all sts.

Sleeves
Using MC and dpn, cast on 24 (26, 30, 32, 32, 36) sts.
Join without twisting, pm between first and last st.
Work even in k1, p1 ribbing for 2 inches, inc 2 (2, 2, 2, 4, 4) sts evenly on last rnd. (26, 28, 32, 34, 36, 40 sts)
Change to larger needles.
Working in Stripe Sequence, inc 1 st each side of marker [every 3rd rnd] 12 (12, 8, 18, 16, 16) times, then [every 4th round] 5 (6, 9, 2, 4, 5) times. (60, 64, 66, 74, 76, 82 sts)
Change to longer needles as necessary.
Work even until sleeve measures 16½ (17½, 17½, 18, 18½, 19½) inches. Bind off all sts.
Sew shoulder seams.

Neck Band
With MC and smaller circular needle, pick up and knit 58 (62, 64, 68, 72, 74) sts around neck edge including sts on holder.
Join, pm between first and last st.
Work in k1, p1 ribbing for 6 rnds.
Bind off loosely in pat.

Assembly
Sew sleeves into armholes.

Dog Sweater

Body

Beg at tail, with MC and smaller needles, cast on 46 sts.

Work even in k1, p1 ribbing for 6 rows.

Change to larger needles.

Work even in Stripe Sequence until body measures 6 inches, ending with a RS row.

Cast on 15 sts at end of last row. (61 sts)

Beg stomach band

Join, pm between first and last st.

Work in rnds until band measures 3 inches, ending 15 sts before marker on last rnd.

Next row: Bind off 15 sts, remove marker work to end of row.

Work even in rows from this point until sweater measures 13 inches.

Change to smaller needles.

With MC only, work even in k1, p1 ribbing for 6 rows.

Beg neck strap

Next row: Bind off 40 sts, work to end of row.

Work even in garter st on rem 6 sts until strap measures 6½ inches or desired length.

Buttonhole row: K2, k2tog, yo, k2.

Work even in garter st for ½ inch more.

Bind off all sts.

Sew on button opposite strap. ■

Day & Night Ensemble

Designs by Scarlet Taylor

Pair this "little black skirt" with the comfortable sweater for a wardrobe essential you'll wear from 9 to 5 and later!

Skill Level

EASY

Size

Woman's extra-small (small, medium, large) Instructions are given for smallest size, with larger sizes in parentheses. When only 1 number is given, it applies to all sizes.

Finished Measurements

Sweater
Chest: 35 (40½, 44, 48) inches
Length: 22½ (23, 23½, 24) inches
Skirt
Hip: 35 (37, 39, 41) inches
Waist (without elastic): 25 (27, 29, 31) inches

Materials

Pullover
- Brown Sheep Lamb's Pride Worsted 85 percent wool/15 percent mohair worsted weight yarn (190 yds/4 oz per skein): 5 (6, 6, 7) skeins sable #M07
- Size 6 (4mm) straight and 16-inch circular needles
- Size 8 (5mm) needles or size needed to obtain gauge

Skirt
- Brown Sheep Lamb's Pride Worsted 85 percent wool/15 percent mohair worsted weight yarn (190 yds/4 oz per skein): 4 (4, 5, 5) skeins onyx #M05
- Size 8 (5mm) 24-inch circular needle or size needed to obtain gauge
- 1 yd (1½-inch-wide) noncurling elastic
- Stitch markers

Gauge

Pullover
17 sts and 24 rows = 4 inches/10cm in St st with larger needles
Skirt
16 sts and 22 rnds = 4 inches/10cm in St st with smaller circular needle
To save time, take time to check gauge.

Special Abbreviation

M1 (Make 1): Insert LH needle under horizontal thread between st just worked and next st, knit through the back. This inc is used for sleeve shaping.

Pattern Note

Shorten or lengthen skirt as desired before placing dec markers.

Pullover

Back

With smaller needles, cast on 74 (86, 94, 102) sts.
Work in k2, p2 rib for 2 inches, ending with a WS row.
Change to larger needles and St st.
Work even until back measures 13½ inches, ending with a WS row.

Shape armholes
Next 2 rows: Bind off 2 (4, 3, 4) sts, work to end of row.
Dec row: K2, ssk, knit to last 4 sts, k2tog, k2.
P 1 row.

[Rep these 2 rows] 0 (1, 1, 2) times more.
(68, 74, 84, 88 sts)
Work even until armhole measures 8 (8½, 9, 9½)
inches, ending with a WS row.

Shape neck

Next row (RS): K20 (23, 28, 28), join 2nd ball of
yarn and bind off center 28 (28, 28, 32) sts, knit
to end of row.

Working on both sides of neck with separate
balls of yarn, dec 1 st at each neck edge on
next row. (19, 22, 27, 27 sts rem each side)

Shape shoulders

At each arm edge, bind off 6 (7, 9, 9) sts twice,
then 7 (8, 9, 9) sts once.

Front

Work as for back until front measures 6¼ (6¾,
7¼, 7¾) inches, ending with a WS row.

Shape neck

Next row (RS): K26 (29, 34, 35), join 2nd ball of
yarn and bind off center 16 (16, 16, 18) sts, knit
to end of row.

Working on both sides of neck with separate
balls of yarn, bind off at each neck edge [3 sts]
1 (1, 1, 2) times, then [2 sts] 1 (1, 1, 0) times.
(21, 24, 27, 27 sts)

Dec row (RS): Knit to last 4 sts of left neck,
k2tog, k2; drop yarn, pick up yarn for right side
of neck, k2, ssk, knit to end of row.

P 1 row, rep dec row. 19 (22, 27, 27) sts rem
each side

Work even until armhole measures same
as for back.

Shape shoulders as for back.

Sew shoulder seams.

Sleeves

With smaller needles, cast on 38 (38, 42, 42) sts.
Work in k2, p2 rib for 2 inches, ending with a
WS row.

Change to larger needles.

Working in St st, inc 1 st each end [every
4th row] 0 (4, 3, 12) times, then [every 6th row]
15 (13, 14, 8) times. (68, 72, 76, 82 sts)

Work even until sleeve measures 19 (18½, 18½,
19) inches, ending with a WS row.

Shape cap

Next 2 rows: Bind off 2 (4, 3, 4) sts, work to
end of row.

Dec row: K2, ssk, knit to last 4 sts, k2tog, k2.
Purl 1 row.

[Rep these 2 rows] 0 (1, 1, 2) times more. (62,
60, 66, 68 sts)

Neck Band

Beg at right shoulder seam with circular needle, pick up and knit 72 (72, 72, 76) sts around neck opening. Join, pm between first and last st. Work even in k2, p2 ribbing for 3½ inches. Bind off in pat.

Assembly

Sew in sleeves.
Sew sleeve and side seams.

Skirt

Beg at hem with circular needle, cast on 176 (184, 196, 204) sts.

Join without twisting, pm between first and last st.

Work even in k2, p2 rib for 1 inch.

Dec rnd—size extra-small and medium only: [K2tog, k3, k2tog, k2] 4 times, [k2tog, k3] 28 (32) times. (140, 156 sts)

Sizes small and large only: [K2tog, k4, k2tog, k3] 3 times, [k2tog, k3] 29 (33) times, k2tog, k4. 148 (164) sts

All sizes: Work even until skirt measures 13½ inches or approx 9½ inches less than desired length.

Shape hips

Next rnd: K28 (29, 33, 34), pm, [k28 (30, 30, 32), pm] 3 times, k28 (29, 33, 34). 5 markers on needle.

Dec rnd: [K2tog, knit to next marker, ssk, knit to next marker] twice, ssk, knit to end of rnd.

Knit 4 rnds.

[Rep last 5 rnds] 7 times more. (100, 108, 116, 124 sts)

Work even until skirt measures 21 inches or desired length.

Beg waistband

Work in k2, p2 rib for 1½ inches.

Purl 1 rnd for turning ridge.

Continue in established rib until waistband measures 3 inches.

Bind off in pat.

Finishing

Fold waistband to inside at turning ridge, forming casing.

Sew waistband in place leaving a 3-inch opening.

Cut elastic to comfortably fit waist when slightly stretched, plus a 1-inch overlap.

Thread elastic through casing. Overlap ends and sew tog securely.

Sew waistband opening. ■

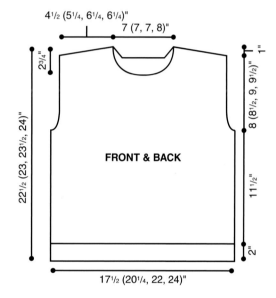

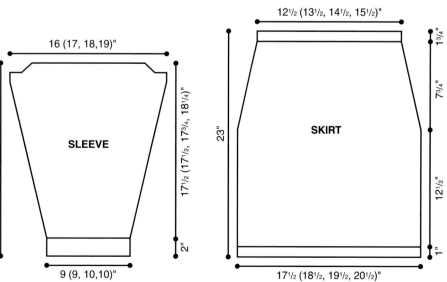

Favorite Teen Turtleneck

Design by Scarlet Taylor

Combine graduated ribbing with Stockinette stitch for a quick-to-knit fashionable sweater your favorite teen will love to wear.

Skill Level
INTERMEDIATE

Size
Woman's extra-small (small, medium, large) Instructions are given for smallest size, with larger sizes in parentheses. When only 1 number is given, it applies to all sizes.

Finished Measurements
Chest: 32 (36, 40, 42) inches
Length: 19½ (19½, 20, 20¾) inches

Materials
- Brown Sheep Lamb's Pride Superwash Worsted 100 percent wool worsted weight yarn (200 yds/100g per skein): 6 (6, 7, 8) skeins sweeten pink #SW35
- Size 5 (3.75mm) needles
- Size 7 (4.5mm) needles or size needed to obtain gauge

Gauge
20 sts and 25 rows = 4 inches/10cm in St st with larger needles
To save time, take time to check gauge.

Special Abbreviation
M1 (Make 1): Insert LH needle under horizontal thread between st just worked and next st, knit in back of st.

Pattern Notes
Selvage sts are worked in St st throughout pat where indicated.
To work fully fashioned dec at armhole edge and sleeve cap on RS rows: K2, ssk, work to last 4 sts, k2tog, k2.
On WS rows: P2, p2tog, work to last 4 sts, p2tog-tbl.
To work fully fashioned dec at neck edge on RS rows: Knit sts at left side of neck until 4 sts rem, k2tog, k2. For right side of neck k2, ssk, knit to end of row.
On WS rows: Purl sts at right side of neck until 4 sts rem, p2tog-tbl, p2. For left side of neck p2, p2tog, purl to end of row.
Sleeve incs are worked as M1.

Back
With larger needles, cast on 82 (92, 102, 107) sts.
Row 1 (RS): K1 (selvage st), *k3, p2; rep from * to last st, k1 (selvage st).
Work even in established rib pat until back measures 2 (2, 2, 2½) inches, ending with a WS row.
Set up Graduated Rib pat (RS): Work rib pat over 27 (32, 32, 37) sts, k 28 (28, 38, 33) sts, work rib pat on rem 27 (32, 32, 37) sts.
Keeping rib pat as established and rem center sts in St st, work even for 11 (9, 9, 7) rows.
Row 12 (10, 10, 8): Rib 22 (27, 27, 32) sts, k 38 (38, 48, 43) sts, rib 22 (27, 27, 32) sts.

Work even in newly established pat for 11 (9, 9, 7) rows.

Row 24 (20, 20, 16): Rib 17 (22, 22, 27), k48 (48, 58, 53), rib 17 (22, 22, 27).

Work even in newly established pat for 11 (9, 9, 7) rows.

Row 36 (30, 30, 24): Rib 12 (17, 17, 22), k58 (58, 68, 63), rib 12 (17, 17, 22).

Work even in newly established pat for 11 (9, 9, 7) rows.

Row 48 (40, 40, 32): Rib 7 (12, 12, 17), k68 (68, 78, 73), rib 7 (12, 12, 17).

Work even in newly established pat for 0 (9, 9, 7) rows.

Sizes small, medium and large only:

Row 50 (50, 40): Rib 7 (7,12), k 78 (88, 83) sts, rib 7 (7, 12) sts.

Size large only: Work even in newly established pat for 7 rows.

Row 48: Rib 7, k93, rib 7.

All sizes: Work even in established pat until back measures approx 11½ inches, ending with a WS row.

Shape armholes

Change to St st.

Bind off 3 (6, 5, 5) sts at beg of next 2 rows, then 0 (0, 4, 4) sts at beg of following 2 rows. (76, 80, 84, 89 sts)

Work 1 fully fashioned dec each end [every

other row] 3 (3, 2, 2) times. (70, 74, 80, 85 sts)

Work even until armhole measures 6¾ (6¾, 7¼, 8) inches, ending with a WS row.

Shape neck

Next row (RS): K19 (21, 24, 26), join 2nd ball of yarn and bind off next 32 (32, 32, 33) sts, work to end of row.

Working on both sides of neck with separate balls of yarn, dec 1 st at each neck edge. 18 (20, 23, 25) sts on each side.

Shape shoulders

At each arm edge, bind off 6 (7, 8, 9) sts twice, then 6 (6, 7, 7) sts once.

Front

Work as for back until armhole measures 5¼ (5¼, 5¾, 6½) inches, ending with a WS row.

Shape neck

Next row (RS): K29 (31, 34, 36), join 2nd ball of yarn and bind off center 12 (12, 12, 13) sts, work to end row.

Working on both sides of neck with separate balls of yarn, bind off 4 sts at each neck edge twice. (21, 23, 26, 28 sts on each side)

Work 1 fully fashioned dec each side of neck [every row] once, then [every other row] twice. (18, 20, 23, 25 sts on each side)

Work even until armhole measures same as for back.

Shape shoulders as for back.

Sleeves

With larger needles, cast on 42 (42, 42, 47) sts.

Set up pat: P1, *k3, p2; rep from * to last st, k1.

Working in established rib pat, inc 1 st each end [every 6th row] 11 (10, 20, 20) times, then [every 8th row] 6 (7, 0, 0) times, working added sts into pat. (76, 76, 82, 87 sts)

Work even until sleeve measures 19¼ (19¾, 20¼, 20¼) inches, ending with a WS row

Shape sleeve cap

Bind off 3 (6, 5, 5) sts at beg of next 2 rows, then 0 (0, 4, 4) sts at beg of following 2 rows. (70, 64, 64, 69 sts)

Work 1 fully fashioned dec each end [every other row] 3 (3, 2, 2) times.
Bind off rem 64 (58, 60, 65) sts.
Sew left shoulder seam.

Collar

With RS facing and using smaller needles, pick up and knit 82 sts evenly around neckline.
Next row (WS): P1, *k2, p3; rep from * to last st, p1.
Work even in established rib pat for 3 inches.
Bind off loosely in pat.

Assembly

Sew rem shoulder seam and collar.
Sew in sleeves.
Sew sleeve and side seams. ◼

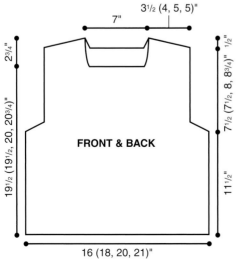

FRONT & BACK

3½ (4, 5, 5)"

7"

2¾"

7½ (7½, 8, 8¾)"

½"

19½ (19½, 20, 20¾)"

11½"

16 (18, 20, 21)"

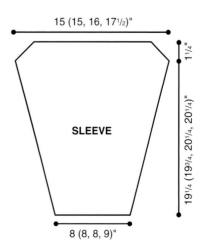

SLEEVE

15 (15, 16, 17½)"

1¼"

19¼ (19¾, 20¼, 20¼)"

8 (8, 8, 9)"

Rugged Sleeveless Jacket

Design by Katharine Hunt

This rugged outdoor vest with zip front, longer back and shaped collar is generously sized for layering.

Skill Level

INTERMEDIATE

Size

Woman's small (medium/large, extra-large) Instructions are given for smallest size, with larger sizes in parentheses. When only 1 number is given, it applies to all sizes.

Finished Measurements

Chest: 39 (45½, 52) inches
Length: 21½ (22½, 24) inches

Materials

- Brown Sheep Burly Spun 100 percent wool super bulky weight yarn (132 yds/8 oz per skein): 4 (4, 5) skeins prairie fire #BS181
- Size 11 (8mm) needles
- Size 13 (9mm) needles or size needed to obtain gauge
- 20 (20, 22)-inch separating zipper

Gauge

10 sts and 15 rows = 4 inches/10cm in Zigzag pat with larger needles
To save time, take time to check gauge.

Special Abbreviation

W&T (Wrap and Turn): Bring yarn to front of work, sl next st purlwise, take yarn to back of work, replace st to LH needle, turn.

Pattern Stitch

Seed
Row 1: *P1, k1; rep from * to last st, p1.
Row 2: Knit the purl sts and purl the knit sts as they present themselves.
Rep Row 2 for pat.

Pattern Note

To minimize jog when binding off shoulder sts, sl the first st of each bound-off section instead of working it. Pass slipped st over next st to bind off.

Left Front

With smaller needles, cast on 24 (28, 32) sts. Change to larger needles.
Work even in Seed st for 4 rows.
Referring to Chart A for chosen size, work even until front measures 12 (12½, 13) inches, ending with a WS row.
Shape armhole
Next row: Bind off 2 (4, 7) sts, work in pat to end of row. (22, 24, 25 sts)
Dec 1 st at arm edge [every other row] 4 times. (18, 20, 21 sts)
Work even until armhole measures 7½ (8, 8½) inches, ending with a RS row.
Shape front neck
Next row: Bind off 5 sts, work in pat to end of row. (13, 15, 16 sts)
Dec 1 st at neck edge [every row] twice, then [every other row] twice. (9, 11, 12 sts)

Work even until armhole measures 9½ (10, 11) inches, ending with a WS row.

Shape shoulders

Bind off at arm edge 3 (3, 4) sts once, then 3 (4, 4) sts twice.

Right Front

Work as for left front, reversing shaping.

Back

With smaller needles, cast on 43 (51, 59) sts. Change to larger needles.

Work in Seed st for 4 rows, inc 1 st at each end of Row 3. (45, 53, 61 sts)

Set up pat: Work Seed st over 5 sts, Row 1 of Chart B over next 40 (48, 56) sts, Seed st over rem 5 sts.

Keeping 5 sts at each end in Seed st, work Rows 2–6 of chart B, inc 1 st each end [every other row] twice. (49, 57, 65 sts)

Working even in Zigzag pat only, rep Rows 7–12 until back measures same as front to underarm.

Shape armholes

Bind off 2 (4, 7) sts at beg of next 2 rows.

Dec 1 st each end [every other row] 4 times. (37, 41, 43 sts)

Work even until armhole measures same as front.

Shape shoulders

Bind off 3 (3, 4) sts at beg of next 2 rows, then 3 (4, 4) sts at beg of following 4 rows.

Bind off rem 19 sts.

Sew shoulder seams.

Armbands

Beg at underarm with RS facing and smaller needle, pick up and knit 61 (63, 67) sts evenly around armhole.

Work in Seed st for 3 rows.

Bind off in pat.

Right Front Edging

With RS facing and smaller needle, pick up and knit 53 (55, 57) sts beg above Seed st border and ending at neck edge.

Bind off knitwise on WS.

Left Front Edging

Beg picking up sts at neck edge.

Work as for right front edging.

Collar

With RS facing and smaller needle, pick up and knit 18 (18, 19) sts along right front neck edge to shoulder; 19 sts across back neck, and 18 (18, 19) sts along left front neck edge. (55, 55, 57 sts)

Work Row 1 of Seed st.

Row 2 (RS): Ssk, Seed st over next 6 sts, W&T.

Row 3: Seed st over 7 sts.

Row 4: Ssk, Seed st over next 13 sts working previous wrap and its st tog, W&T.

Row 5: Seed st over 14 sts.

Row 6: Ssk, work in pat to last 2 sts working previous wrap and its st tog, k2tog. (51, 51, 53 sts)
Row 7: Seed st over 7 sts, W&T.
Row 8: Work in pat to last 2 sts, k2 tog. (50, 50, 52 sts)
Row 9: Seed st over 14 sts, W&T.
Row 10: Rep Row 8. (49, 49, 51 sts)
Row 11: Work in pat across all sts. Bind off in pat.

Finishing

Sew zipper to front edges
Sew side seams. ■

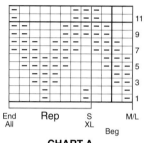

CHART A
LEFT FRONT

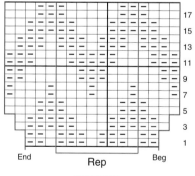

CHART B
BACK

STITCH KEY
☐ K on RS, p on WS
⊟ P on RS, k on WS

Rodeo Vest

Design by Pauline Schultz

This vest will add a cozy layer for those "cowboy chic" occasions.

Skill Level

INTERMEDIATE

Size
Woman's small (medium, large, extra-large)
Instructions are given for smallest size, with
larger sizes in parentheses. When only
1 number is given, it applies to all sizes.

Finished Measurements
Chest: 36 (40, 44, 48) inches
Length: 23 (23¼, 23½, 23¾) inches

Materials
• Brown Sheep Burly Spun 100 percent wool super bulky weight yarn
  (132 yds/8 oz per skein): 3 (3, 4, 4)
  skeins oatmeal #BS115 (MC)
• Brown Sheep Nature Spun Worsted
  100 percent wool worsted weight
  yarn (245 yds/100g per skein):
  1 skein Bev's bear #N94 (CC)
• Size 4 (3.5mm) double-pointed needles
  (2 only)
• Size 13 (9mm) 32-inch circular needle or
  size needed to obtain gauge
• 2 (1⅛-inch) buttons
• Stitch markers
• Stitch holders
• Small amount worsted weight yarn to
  match MC

Gauge
9 sts and 17 rows = 4 inches/10cm in Seed st
with larger needles
To save time, take time to check gauge.

Pattern Stitch
Seed Stitch
Row 1: *K1, p1; rep from * across.
Row 2: Knit the purl sts, and purl the knit sts.
Rep Row 2 for pat.

Pattern Note
Circular needles are used to accommodate
large number of sts. Do not join; work in rows.

Body
With MC and larger needle, cast on 64 (70, 78,
84) sts.
Work 1 row in Seed St pat.
Working in established pat, inc 1 st each end
[every row] 3 (5, 5, 5) times, then [every other
row] 3 (4, 4, 5) times, and finally [every 3rd row]
twice. (80, 92, 100, 108 sts)
Pm after sts 20 (23, 25, 27) and 60 (69, 75, 81).
Work even until body measures 15 (15, 15,
15½) inches, ending with a WS row.
Divide for fronts and back
[Work to 2 (4, 6, 6) sts before marker, bind off
4 (8, 12, 12) sts for underarm] twice, work to
end of row.
Remove markers, place sts for back and right
front on holders.

Left Front
Dec 1 st at arm edge [every other row] 2 (2, 2,
3) times. (16, 17, 17, 18 sts)
Work even until armhole measures 5 (5¼, 5½,
5¾) inches.
Inc 1 st at arm edge [every other row] 2 (2, 3, 3)
times. (18, 19, 20, 21 sts)

Work even until armhole measures 7 (7¼, 7½, 7¾) inches, ending at arm edge.

Shape shoulders
At arm edge, bind off 5 (6, 6, 6) sts twice, then 1 st [every row] 4 (3, 4, 5) times, *at the same time*, dec 1 st at neck edge [every other row] 4 times.

Right Front
With WS facing, join yarn at arm edge.
Work as for left front, reversing shaping.

Back
With WS facing, join yarn at left underarm and work across row.
Dec 1 st at each end [every other row] 2 (2, 2, 3) times. (32, 34, 34, 36 sts)
Work even until armhole measures 5 (5¼, 5½, 5¾) inches.
Inc 1 st at each end [every other row] 2 (2, 3, 3) times. (36, 38, 40, 42 sts)
Work even until armhole measures 7 (7¼, 7½, 7¾) inches, ending at arm edge.

Shape shoulders
Bind off 5 (6, 6, 6) sts at beg next 4 rows.
Dec 1 st each end [every row] twice.
Bind off rem 12 (10, 12, 14) sts.

I-Cord Button Loops
Make 2
With CC and dpn, cast on 4 sts, leaving a 6-inch tail.
*K4, slide sts to opposite end of needle; rep from * until cord measures 7 inches.
Cut yarn, leaving a 6-inch end.
Draw end through sts and pull tight.

Finishing
Sew shoulder seams using matching lighter weight yarn.
With 2 strands of CC, referring to Fig. 1, work blanket stitch around armholes and body.

Fig. 1
Blanket Stitch

Mark positions of 2 button lps on right front, having one level with underarm and another 2 inches above first.
Position lps by poking ends through fabric to opposite side. Sew ends in place.
Sew on buttons. ■

Easy Zoom Jacket

Design by Kennita Tully

Reverse Stockinette stitch and naturally rolled edges add a trendy look to a short jacket.

Skill Level

EASY

Size

Woman's small (medium, large, extra-large) Instructions are given for smallest size, with larger sizes in parentheses. When only 1 number is given, it applies to all sizes.

Finished Measurements

Chest: 38 (42, 46, 50) inches
Length: 18 (19, 20, 21) inches

Materials

- Brown Sheep Prairie Silks 72 percent wool/18 percent mohair/10 percent silk worsted weight yarn (88 yds/50g per hank): 10 (11, 12, 13) hanks green back #PS850
- Size 8 (5mm) needles or size needed to obtain gauge
- 3 (1-inch) buttons
- Stitch markers

Gauge

16 sts and 24 rows = 4 inches/10cm in reverse St st
To save time, take time to check gauge.

Pattern Notes

All incs are worked 1 st from edge by making a backwards lp and placing on RH needle.
If desired, sleeves may be worked cuffed back.

Back

Cast on 78 (86, 94, 102) sts.
Work even in reverse St st until back measures 9½ (10, 10½, 11) inches, ending with a WS row.

Shape armhole

Next 2 rows: Bind off 8 (9, 10, 12) sts, work to end of row. (62, 68, 74, 78 sts)
Work even until armhole measures 8½ (9, 9½, 10) inches.
Bind off all sts.
Mark center 28 (30, 32, 34) sts for back neck.

Left Front

Cast on 44 (48, 52, 56) sts.

Work even in reverse St st until front measures 9½ (10, 10½, 11) inches, ending with a WS row.

Shape armhole

Next row (RS): Bind off 8 (9, 10, 12) sts, work to end of row. (36, 39, 42, 44 sts)

Work even until armhole measures same as for back.

Shape shoulder and back collar

Next row (RS): Bind off 17 (19, 21, 22) sts, work to end of row.

Work even on rem 19 (20, 21, 22) sts until collar measures 3½ (3¾, 4, 4¼) inches.

Bind off.

Right Front

Work as for left front, except work armhole and shoulder bind-off rows on WS of work.

At the same time, make 3 buttonholes, having first one 3½ (3½, 4, 4) inches from lower edge and spacing rem 3½ inches apart.

Buttonhole row (RS): P3, bind off 3 sts, purl to end of row. On following row, cast on 3 sts over previously bound-off sts.

Sleeves

Cast on 36 (38, 40, 42) sts.

Work in reverse St st, inc 1 st each end [every 6th row] 6 (10, 14, 18) times, then [every 8th row] 10 (7, 4, 1) times. (68, 72, 76, 80 sts)

Mark each st of last row for underarm.

Work even for 2 (2¼, 2½, 3) inches more.

Bind off all sts.

Assembly

Sew shoulder seams.

Sew short ends of collar sections tog at center back.

Sew long edge of collar to back neck.

Fold collar to outside and tack to back neck between shoulders

Sew sleeves into armholes, matching markers to first bound-off st of underarm.

Sew sleeve and side seams.

Sew on buttons. ■

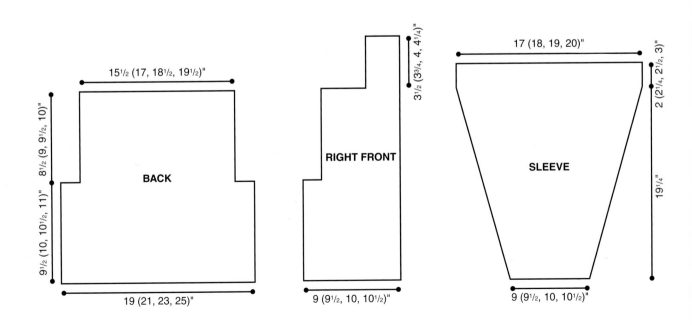

Rainbow Poncho

Design by Bonnie Franz

All the colors in the rainbow (plus pink) are included in this poncho that will brighten up even the dreariest day.

Skill Level

BEGINNER

Size

Woman's small (medium, large) Instructions are given for smallest size, with larger sizes in parentheses. When only 1 number is given, it applies to all sizes.

Finished Measurements

Shoulder: 19 (22, 24) inches
Front edge: 27 (29, 32) inches

Materials

- Brown Sheep Lamb's Pride Superwash Bulky, 100 percent wool bulky weight yarn (110 yds/100g per skein): 9 (10, 11) skeins alabaster #SW10 (MC), 1 skein each sweeten pink #SW35 (A), red wing #SW01 (B), blaze #SW145 (C), saffron #SW14 (D), emerald city #SW52 (E), cornflower #SW57 (F), sapphire #SW65 (G), amethyst #SW62 (H)
- Size 10½ (6.5mm) 36-inch circular needle or size needed to obtain gauge

Gauge

14 sts and 22 rows = 4 inches/10cm in Color Stripe pat
To save time, take time to check gauge.

Pattern Stitch
Color Stripe

Rows 1, 2, 3, 5, 7 and 8: With MC, knit.
Rows 4 and 6: With MC, purl.
Rows 9 and 10: With CC, knit.
Rep Rows 1–10 in this CC color order: A, B, C, D, E, F, G, H.

Pattern Note

Do not cut MC when working CC; carry up side of work.

Small Section

Using MC, cast on 56 sts.
Work even in Color Stripe pat until piece measures 19 (22, 24) inches.
Bind off.

Large Section

Using MC, cast on 189 (204, 224) sts.
Work even in Color Stripe pat until piece measures 19 (22, 24) inches.
Bind off.

Assembly

Sew side edge of small section to cast-on edge of larger section (Fig. 1).
Leaving center section of cast-on edge free, sew rem side of small section to cast-on edge of larger section.

Fringe

Cut lengths of yarn, each 10 inches long.
Fold 2 strands of the same color in half and pull through corresponding stripe color on short ends of large section and knot.
Rep fringe around remainder of poncho.
Trim fringe even. ■

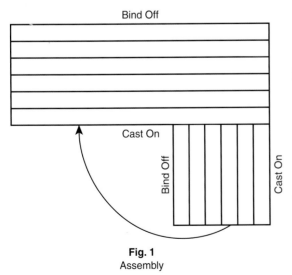

Fig. 1
Assembly

Evening Heather Poncho

Design by Katharine Hunt

Four easy rectangles, seamed at the center back and shoulders, create a casual and cozy garment. The earthy stripes are reminiscent of primitive woven panels.

Skill Level

EASY

Size
One size fits most

Finished Measurements
Width: 40½ inches
Length from top of shoulder: 31 inches

Materials
- Brown Sheep Burly Spun 100 percent wool super bulky yarn (132 yds/ 8 oz per skein): 6 skeins grey heather #BS03 (MC), 2 skeins charcoal heather #BS04 (CC)
- Size 13 (9mm) needles or size needed to obtain gauge

SUPER BULKY 6

Gauge
10 sts and 14 rows = 4 inches/10cm in St st
To save time, take time to check gauge.

Special Abbreviation
W&T (Wrap & Turn): Bring yarn to front of work, sl next st purlwise, take yarn to back of work, replace sl st to LH needle, turn.

Pattern Stitch
Seed Stitch
Row 1 (RS): P1, *k1, p1; rep from * across.

Row 2: Knit the purl sts and purl the knit sts as they present themselves.
Rep Row 2 for pat.

Pattern Notes
All Seed st sections on left front and right back beg and end with k1. On right front and left back, they beg and end with p1.

The first row of each wide CC Seed st stripe is worked in St st.

Left Front

With MC, cast on 49 sts.
Referring to Chart A, work in Seed st and stripe pat as shown until Row 92 has been completed.
Beg Seed st of fold-back collar area on following row, *at the same time*, beg shoulder

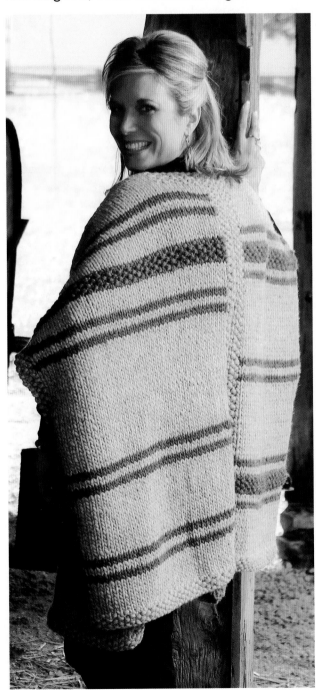

shaping on Row 104 as follows:

Short-row shoulder shaping

Rows 1 (WS)–2: Work to last 8 sts, W&T, work to end of row.

Rows 3–4: Work to last 16 sts, W&T, work to end of row.

Rows 5–6: Work to last 24 sts, W&T, work to end of row.

Row 7: Bind off 8 sts for edge of collar, work to end of row, hiding wraps.
Bind off all sts.

Right Front

Referring to Chart B for stripe pat, work as for left front reversing shoulder shaping.

Right Back

Work as for left front, until Row 103 has been completed.
Work shoulder shaping and Seed st of back neck band as shown on Chart C.

Left Back

Work as for right front, until Row 104 has been completed.
Work shoulder shaping and Seed st of back neck band as shown on Chart D.

Assembly

Sew center back seam.
Sew shoulder seams.

Braided Tassels
Make 2

Cut 3 strands of MC, each 22 inches long.
Pull strands through top corner of fold-back collar, and center them evenly.
Braid tightly, using 2 strands for each section.
Wrap bottom of braid with a short strand of yarn to secure end. Tie tightly.
Trim ends even, then "comb" ends with fingers to remove the twist and fluff ends. ■

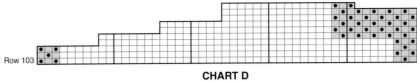

CHART D
LEFT BACK

STITCH & COLOR KEY
- ☐ MC St st
- ● MC Seed st
- − CC Seed st
- ◇ CC St st

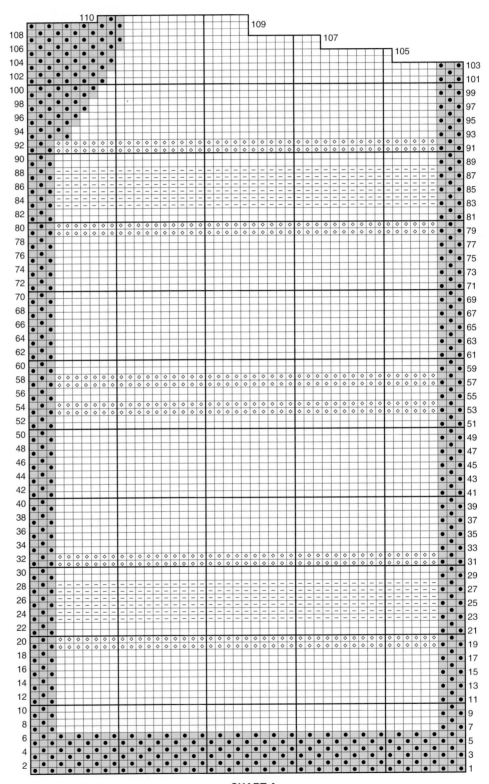

CHART A
LEFT FRONT

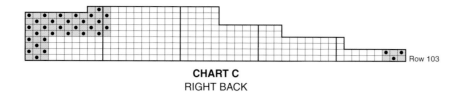

CHART C
RIGHT BACK

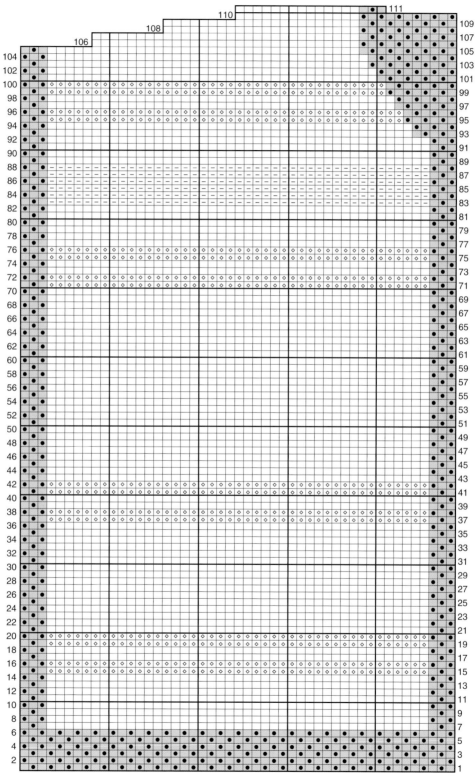

CHART B
RIGHT FRONT

Comfy Cozy Hoodie

Design by Katharine Hunt

A very warm outdoor jacket with zip front and hood is sure to please both man and woman. Three colors held together give a marl effect to the basket-weave pattern.

Skill Level

◼◼◼◻
INTERMEDIATE

Size

Adult small (medium, large) Instructions are given for smallest size, with larger sizes in parentheses. When only 1 number is given, it applies to all sizes.

Finished Measurements

Chest (closed): 40 (44, 48) inches
Length: 22 (23, 24) inches

Materials

- Brown Sheep Nature Spun 100 percent wool worsted weight yarn (245 yds/100g per skein): 4 (5, 6) skeins each Peruvian pink #N85 (A), meadow green #N56 (B) and sapphire #N65 (C)
- Size 10½ (6.5mm) straight and 24-inch circular needles
- Size 11 (8mm) needles or size needed to obtain gauge
- 20 (20, 22)-inch separating zipper

4 MEDIUM

Gauge

12 sts and 19 rows = 4 inches/10cm in pat with larger needles
To save time, take time to check gauge.

Special Abbreviations

M1 (Make 1): Make a backwards lp and place on RH needle.

Wrap: Bring yarn to front of work, sl next st from LH needle purlwise to RH needle, take yarn to back of work, replace sl st to LH needle.

Pattern Stitch

Basket Weave (multiple of 12 sts + 7)
Rows 1, 3 and 5 (RS): P7, *k5, p7; rep from * across row.
Rows 2, 4 and 6: K7, *p5, k7; rep from * across row.
Rows 7, 9 and 11: P1, *k5, p7; rep from *, end last rep p6.
Rows 8, 10 and 12: K6, *p5, k7; rep from *, end last rep k1.
Rep Rows 1–12 for pat.

Pattern Notes

Garment is worked with 1 strand each color held tog throughout.
Front edgings are worked with 1 strand each of A and B.
Seams are sewn with 1 strand each of A and B.

Back

With smaller needles, cast on 61 (67, 73) sts.
Work in k1, p1 ribbing for 1½ inches, ending with a WS row.
Change to larger needles.
Set up pat
Size small only: K3, work in pat over next 55 sts, k3.
Size medium only: P1, k5, work in pat over next 55 sts, k5, p1.

Size large only: P4, k5, work in pat over next 55 sts, k5, p4.

All sizes: Work even in established Basket Weave pat until back measures 12½ (13, 13½) inches, ending with a WS row.

Shape armhole

Bind off 9 sts at beg of next 2 rows. (43, 49, 55 sts)

Work even until armhole measures 8½ (9, 9½) inches, ending with a WS row.

Shape shoulders and back neck

Next 2 rows: Work in pat to last 3 (5, 6) sts, wrap next st, turn.

Mark center 19 (21, 21) sts.

Next row: Work to first marker, join 2nd ball of yarn and bind off marked sts, remove markers, work to last 7 (9, 11) sts, wrap next st, turn, work to 2 sts before neckline, work last 2 sts tog.

Drop yarn, pick up 2nd ball, dec 1 st at neck edge, work to last 7 (9, 11) sts, wrap next st, turn, work to neck edge.

Working on both sides, work 1 row even working wraps and parent sts tog.

Bind off all sts.

Left Front

With smaller needles, cast on 30 (33, 36) sts. Work in k1, p1 ribbing as for back. Change to larger needles.

Set up pat

Size small only: K3, work in pat to end of row.

Size medium only: P1, k5, work in pat to end of row.

Size large only: P4, k5, work in pat to end of row.

All sizes: Work even in established Basket Weave pat until front measures same as back to underarm, ending with a WS row.

Shape armhole

Bind off 9 sts at beg of next row. (21, 24, 27 sts)

Work even until armhole measures 6½ (7, 7) inches, ending with a RS row.

Shape front neck

Next row (WS): Bind off 4 sts, work in pat to end of row. (17, 20, 23 sts)

Dec 1 st at neck edge [every row] 6 (7, 7) times. (11, 13, 16 sts)

Work even until armhole measures same as for back, ending with a RS row.

Shape shoulder

Work to last 3 (5, 6) sts, wrap next st, turn, work to end of row.

Work to last 7 (9, 11) sts, wrap next st, turn, work to end of row.

Work across all sts working wraps and parent sts tog.

Bind off all sts.

Right Front

Work as for left front, reversing shaping.

Sew shoulder seams.

Sleeves

With smaller needles cast on 27 (29, 31) sts. Work in k1, p1 ribbing as for back. Change to larger needles.

Set up pat

Next row (RS): P5 (6, 7), k5, p7, k5, p5 (6, 7).

Working in established Basket Weave pat, inc 1 st each end [every 4th row] 9 times, then

[every 6th row] 5 (5, 4) times and finally [every 10th row] 0 (0, 1) time. (55, 57, 59 sts)
Work even until sleeve measures 18¾ (19¼, 19¾) inches.
Mark each end st for underarm.
Work even for ¾ inch more.
Bind off in pat.

Left Front Edging
Beg at neck with smaller circular needle and 1 strand each of A and B held tog, pick up and knit 89 (94, 97) sts along left front edge.
Next row: Bind off all sts.

Right Front Edging
Beg at lower edge, work as for left edging.

Hood
Left Half
Cast on 2 sts.
Row 1 (WS): P1, M1, p1.
Row 2: K1, M1, k2. Mark last st as neck edge.
Row 3: P3, M1, p1. (5 sts)
Change to larger needles.
Working in St st, continue to inc at neck edge until there are 10 sts on needle.
Next row (WS): Purl to end of row, cast on 14 (15, 16) sts. (24, 25, 26 sts)
Inc 1 st at neck edge [every 4th row] 3 times. (27, 28, 29 sts)
Work even for 20 (22, 24) rows.
Shape top of hood
Dec row (RS): K1, ssk, knit to end of row.
Work 3 rows even; rep dec row.
Dec 1 st at shaped edge [every other row] 6 times, then [every row] 6 times.
Bind off rem 15 (16, 17) sts.

Right Half
Work as for left half of hood, reversing shaping.
Sew back seam of hood.

Band
With RS facing and circular needle, pick up and knit 105 (107, 111) sts along front edge of hood.
Work even in k1, p1 ribbing for 4 rows.
Bind off in pat.

Assembly
Insert zipper so that front edges meet and conceal teeth.
Sew hood in place, easing around neck shaping.
Sew in sleeves, matching underarm markers to first bound-off st of underarm.
Sew side and underarm sleeves. ▪

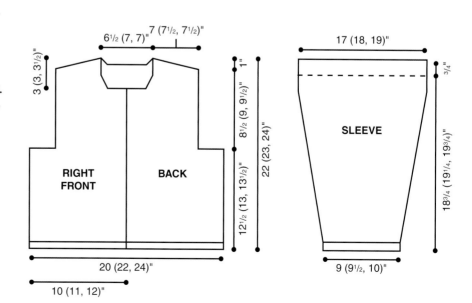

Sideways Stripes

Design by Cindy Polfer

You can never have too many vests; this one is knit from side to side.

Skill Level
◼◼◼▢
INTERMEDIATE

Size
Woman's small (medium, large, extra-large)
Instructions are given for smallest size,
with larger sizes in parentheses. When only
1 number is given, it applies to all sizes.

Finished Measurements
Chest: 42 (46, 50, 54) inches
Armhole depth: 10½ (10¾, 11¼, 11¾) inches
Total length: 23 (23½, 24, 24½) inches

Materials
- Brown Sheep Lamb's Pride
  Superwash Bulky, 100 percent wool
  bulky weight yarn (110 yds/100g
  per skein): 4 (5, 5, 5) skeins combustion grey
  #SW40, 3 (4, 4, 4) skeins each onyx #SW05
  and red baron #SW81
- Size 11 (8mm) needle (1 only)
- Size 13 (9mm) needles or size needed to
  obtain gauge
- Size K/10½ (6.5mm) crochet hook
- Stitch holders
- Stitch markers
- 5 (1-inch) shank buttons
- 5 (½-inch) flat buttons
- Small amount worsted weight waste yarn

Gauge
10 sts = 4 inches/10cm in Stripes pat with
larger needle
24 rows (1 pat rep) = 5¾ inches
To save time, take time to check gauge.

Special Method
Provisional Cast On: With waste yarn and
crochet hook, very loosely ch number of
required sts. With garment yarn, pick up 1 st
in each "bump" on underside of ch.

Pattern Stitch
Stripes
Rows 1 and 2: With CC, knit.
Row 3: With MC, knit.
Row 4: With MC, purl.
Rows 5–8: With CC, knit.
Row 9: With MC, knit.
Row 10: With MC, purl.
Rows 11 and 12: With CC, knit.
Row 13: With MC, knit.
Row 14: With MC, purl.
Row 15: With MC, knit.
Row 16: With MC, purl.
Rows 17–20: With CC, knit.
Row 21: With MC, knit.
Row 22: With MC, purl.
Row 23: With MC, knit.
Row 24: With MC, purl.
Rep Rows 1–24 for pat.

Pattern Notes
Two strands of yarn are held tog throughout
vest. MC is 2 strands gray; CC is 1 strand each
onyx and red.
Fronts of vest are worked at the same time.
Except as noted, instructions apply to both left
and right front.
Fronts are worked from center to side seam;
back is knit from left seam to right seam.
A provisional cast on is used for the back to

provide open sts to be picked up for armhole band and side seam.

Side seams are joined with a unique technique to add stability and lessen bulk at underarms.

Front Band

Using long-tail method with CC and larger needles, cast on 51 (52, 52, 53) sts.

Rows 1 and 2: With CC, knit.

Rows 3: With MC, knit.

Row 4 (left front only): With MC, knit.

Row 4 (right front only): K3 (4, 4, 4) [yo, k2tog, k9] 4 times, yo, k2tog, k2 (2, 2, 3).

Rows 5–8: With CC, knit.

Beg body

With MC and working in St st, bind off 2 sts at beg of next 2 rows. (47, 48, 48, 49 sts)

Left front only: Mark end of first St st row as RS and neck edge.

Right front only: Mark beg of first St st row as RS and neck edge.

Shape neck

Beg with Row 1 of Stripes pat, inc 1 st at neck edge [every 2 (2, 2, 3) rows] 5 (5, 6, 5) times. (52, 53, 54, 54 sts)

Work even ending at neck edge with Row 11 (11, 13, 15) for left front and Row 10 (12, 12, 14) for right front.

Both fronts: With CC (CC, MC, MC) cast 4 (4, 4, 5) sts at neck edge. (56, 57, 58, 59 sts)

Work even, ending with Row 22 (24, 2, 4) of Stripes pat.

Shape armhole

Left front only: Work across 34 (35, 36, 36) sts, place rem 22 (22, 22, 23) sts on holder for armhole edge.

Right front only: Cut yarn. Sl next 22 (22, 22, 23) sts to holder. Attach yarn and work to end of row on rem 34 (35, 36, 36) sts.

Both fronts: Dec 1 st at armhole edge [every other row] 5 (6, 7, 7) times. (29 sts)

Work even until Row 14 (18, 22, 2) of pat is complete.

Place all sts on holders.

Back

With MC (CC, MC, CC) using provisional method and larger needles, cast on 29 sts. Mark end of cast on row as armhole edge.

Beg with Row 24 (20, 16, 12) of Stripes pat, work even until Row 4 (24, 20, 18) is complete.

Shape armhole

Inc 1 st at armhole edge [every 2 (2, 2, 3) rows] 5 (6, 7, 7) times. (34, 35, 36, 36 sts)

Work even until Row 15 (13, 11, 9) of pat is complete, ending at armhole.

Using provisional cast on, with MC (MC, CC, MC) cast on 22 (22, 22, 23) sts. (56, 57, 58, 59 sts)

Beg with Row 16 (14, 12, 10), work even until Row 2 (1, 24, 22) is complete, ending at bottom (neck, bottom, bottom) edge.

Shape back neck

Dec 1 st at neck edge [every row] 4 times. (52, 53, 54, 55 sts)

Work even in pat for 24 (26, 28, 32) rows ending at neck (bottom, neck, neck) edge with Row 7 (8, 9, 11).

Inc 1 st at neck edge [every row] 4 times.
Work even until Row 22 (24, 2, 4) is complete, ending at bottom edge.

Shape armhole
Work armhole shaping as for left front.
Sew shoulder seams.

Left Armband
With larger needles beg at underarm with CC and RS facing, pick up and knit 10 (11, 12, 13) sts at underarm, from holder k20 (20, 20, 21), ssk, remove provisional cast on and place resulting sts on LH needle, knit these 21 (21, 21, 22) sts, pick up and knit 10 (11, 12, 13) sts at underarm. (62, 64, 66, 68 sts)
Knit 2 rows.
Bind off knitwise.

Right Armband
Work as for left armband.

Assembly
Sl sts from left front to larger needle.
Remove provisional cast on from back and place sts on 2nd needle. Do not join yarn.
With RS tog and smaller needle, sl first st of front needle knitwise, sl first st of back needle purlwise, pass first st over 2nd. (1 st on RH needle)
*Sl next set of front and back sts to RH needle, pass 2nd st over 3rd st. (2 sts on RH needle)
Rep from *, slipping sts in this manner until there are 28 sts on RH needle, knit last st.
Turn, join yarn and bind off all sts in normal manner with larger needle.
Rep for right seam.

Neck Band
Beg next to left front band with RS facing using CC and larger needles, pick up and knit 13 (14, 15, 16) sts from left front neck, 20 (21, 22, 23) sts along back, and 13 (14, 15, 16) sts from right front neck. (46, 49, 52, 55 sts)
Knit 2 rows.
Bind off knitwise.
Sew edges of neck band to front band.

Bottom Band
With CC and larger needles, pick up and knit 98 (108, 118, 128) sts along bottom between front bands.
Knit 2 rows.
Bind off knitwise.
Sew edges of bottom band to front band.
Sew on buttons, using smaller button on inside of band for stability. ■

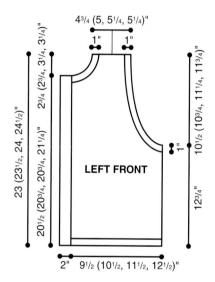

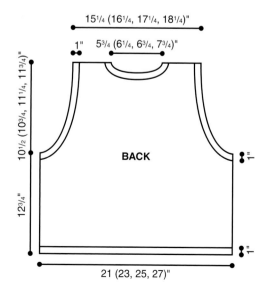

Checkered Cardi

Design by Sandi Prosser

Intarsia blocks enhance the fronts of an elegant cardigan. The motifs are repeated as a band around the back and at lower sleeve edges.

Skill Level

INTERMEDIATE

Size
Woman's small (medium, large, extra-large) Instructions are given for smallest size, with larger sizes in parentheses. When only 1 number is given, it applies to all sizes.

Finished Measurements
Chest (buttoned): 36½ (40, 43, 46) inches
Length: 21 (21, 22½, 23½) inches

Materials
- Brown Sheep Handpaint Originals 70 percent mohair/30 percent worsted weight yarn (88 yds/50g per skein): 10 (10, 11,12) skeins plum purple #HP45 (MC), 4 (4, 5, 5) skeins strawberry patch #HP40 (CC)
- Size 5 (3.75mm) needles
- Size 6 (4mm) needles or size needed to obtain gauge
- Stitch holders
- 7 (⅜-inch) buttons

Gauge
20 sts and 26 rows = 4 inches/10cm in st st with larger needles
To save time, take time to check gauge.

Pattern Stitch
Seed Stitch
Row 1 (RS): *K1, p1; rep from * across.
Row 2: *P1, k1; rep from * across.

Rep Rows 1–2 for pat.

Pattern Notes
Block pat is worked using intarsia method. Wind a separate ball or bobbin for each color section. To avoid holes when changing colors, always bring new color up over old.

Back
With CC and smaller needles, cast on 90 (98, 106, 114) sts.
Work even in Seed st for 5 rows. Change to larger needles.
Row 1 (RS): K5 (9, 5, 9) CC, *k8 MC, k8 CC; rep from *, end last rep k5 (9, 5, 9) MC.
Row 2: P5 (9, 5, 9) CC, *p8 MC, p8 CC; rep from *, end last rep p5 (9, 5, 9) MC.
Rows 3–10: Rep Rows 1 and 2.
Row 11: K5 (9, 5, 9) MC, *k8 CC, k8 MC; rep from *, end last rep k5 (9, 5, 9) CC.
Row 12: P5 (9, 5, 9) MC, *p8 CC, p8 MC; rep from *, end last rep p5 (9, 5, 9) CC.
Rows 13–20: Rep Rows 11 and 12.
Rep Rows 1–10. Cut CC.
Work even in MC only until back measures 13 (13, 13½, 14) inches, ending with a WS row.
Shape armholes
Bind off 4 sts at beg of next 2 rows. (82, 90, 98, 106 sts)
Work even until armhole measures 8 (8, 9, 9½) inches, ending with a WS row.
Shape shoulders
Bind off 10 (12, 13, 15) sts at beg of next 4 rows.
Bind off rem 42 (42, 46, 46) sts.

Right Front

With CC and smaller needles, cast on 46 (50, 54, 58) sts.

Work in Seed st for 5 rows. Change to larger needles.

Set up pat (RS): K1 (9, 1, 9) CC, *k8 MC, k8 CC; rep from *, end last rep k1 CC (k4 CC, k1 MC, k9 MC).

Work even in established color-block pat until front measures same as for back to underarm.

Shape armhole

Next row (WS): Bind off 4 sts, work to end of row. (42, 46, 50, 54 sts)

Work even until armhole measures 4½ (4½, 5, 5) inches, ending with a WS row.

Shape neck

Next row: Bind off 8 (8, 10, 10) sts, work to end of row. (34, 38, 40, 44 sts)

Work 1 row even.

Dec 1 st at neck edge [every row] 14 times. (20, 24, 26, 30 sts)

Work even until armhole measures same as for back.

Shape shoulders

Bind off at arm edge 10 (12, 13, 15) sts twice.

Left Front

Work as for right front until Seed border is complete. Change to larger needles.

Set up pat on next RS row as follows:

Size small only: K5 MC, *k8 CC, k8 MC; rep from *, end last rep k1 MC.

Size medium only: K9 CC, *k8 MC, k8 CC; rep from *, end last rep k1 CC.

Size large only: K5 MC, *k8 CC, k8 MC; rep from *, end last rep k9 MC.

Size extra-large only: K9 CC, *k8 MC, k8 CC; rep from *, end last rep k1 MC.

Continuing in established color-block pat, work as for right front reversing shaping.

Sew shoulder seams.

Neck Band

With RS facing, using smaller needles and CC, pick up and knit 36 sts along right neck edge, knit across 42 (42, 44, 44) sts from back neck st holder, pick up and knit 36 sts along left neck edge. (114, 114, 116, 116 sts)

Work 3 rows in Seed st.

Bind off all sts in pat.

Sleeves

With CC and smaller needles, cast on 48 sts. Work as for right front until Seed border is complete. Change to larger needles.

Set up pat

Next row (RS): K8 CC, k8 MC; rep from * across.

Work even in established color-block pat until 3 rows of blocks have been completed. Cut CC. Working in MC only, inc 1 st each end [every 4th row] 10 (10, 14, 16) times, then [every 6th row] 7 times. (82, 82, 90, 94 sts)

Work even until sleeve measures 18½ (18½, 19½, 19½) inches.

Shape sleeve cap

Mark each end st of last row for underarm.

Work even for 6 more rows.

Bind off 6 sts at the beg of next 6 rows.

Bind off rem 46 (46, 54, 58) sts.

Button Band

With RS facing, using smaller needles and CC, pick up and knit 100 sts evenly along left front edge.
Work 3 rows in Seed st.
Bind off in pat.

Buttonhole Band

With CC and smaller needles, pick up and knit 100 sts evenly along right front edge.
Work 1 row in Seed st.
Next row (RS): Work in pat across 2 sts, *k2tog, yo, pat 14 sts; rep from * to last 4 sts, k2tog, yo, pat 2 sts.
Work 1 row in Seed st.
Bind off in pat.

Assembly

Sew sleeves into armholes, matching underarm marker to first bound-off st of underarm.
Sew side and sleeve seams.
Sew on buttons. ■

Flirty in Lime

Design by Scarlet Taylor

Dainty seed stitch, bell sleeves and a lively lime color make a flirty combination in a cardigan your teenager will love!

Skill Level
■■□□
EASY

Size
Woman's extra-small (small, medium, large)
Instructions are given for smallest size, with larger sizes in parentheses. When only 1 number is given, it applies to all sizes.

Finished Measurements
Chest: 35½ (39, 41, 45½) inches
Length: 21 (21, 22½, 23) inches

Materials
- Brown Sheep Lamb's Pride Bulky 85 percent wool/15 percent mohair bulky weight yarn (125 yds/4 oz per skein): 8 (9, 10, 11) skeins limeade #M120
- Size 8 (5mm) needles
- Size 10½ (6.5mm) needles or size needed to obtain gauge
- 1 (1-inch) button, La Mode #34575
- Tapestry needle

Gauge
14 sts and 24 rows = 4 inches/10cm in Seed st with larger needles
To save time, take time to check gauge.

Special Abbreviations
Ssp-b: Sl 2 sts knitwise 1 at a time, return these 2 sts to LH needle keeping them twisted, purl these 2 sts tog through the back lps.
M1 (Make 1): Insert LH needle under horizontal bar between st just worked and next st, knit through the back.

Pattern Stitch
Seed Stitch (even number of stitches)
Row 1 (RS): *K1, p1, rep from * across.
Row 2: *P1, k1, rep from * across.
Rep Rows 1 and 2 for pat.

Back
With smaller needles, cast on 62 (68, 72, 80) sts.
Work in garter st for 1 inch, ending with a WS row.
Change to larger needles.
Work even in Seed st until back measures 13 (13, 14, 14) inches, ending with a WS row.
Shape armholes
Next 2 rows: Bind off 4 (4, 4, 6) sts, work to end of row. (54, 60, 64, 68 sts)
Work even until armhole measures 8 (8, 8½, 9) inches, ending with a WS row.
Bind off in pat.

Left Front
With smaller needles, cast on 32 (34, 36, 40) sts.
Work even in garter st for 1 inch, ending with a WS row.
Change to larger needles.
Work even in Seed st until front measures same as for back to underarm, ending with a WS row.
Shape armhole
Next row (WS): Bind off 4 (4, 4, 6) sts, work to end of row. (28, 30, 32, 34 sts)

Work even until armhole measures 3 (3, 3½, 4) inches, ending with a RS row.

Shape neck

At neck edge, bind off 3 sts once, then 2 sts once. (23, 25, 27, 29 sts)

Dec row (RS): Work to last 3 sts, k2tog, k1.

Rep dec row [every other row] twice more, then [every 4th row] 4 times. (16, 18, 20, 22 sts)

Work even until armhole measures same as back to shoulders.

Bind off in pat.

Right Front

Work as for left front to neck shaping, working armhole shaping on a RS row and ending with a WS row.

Shape neck

At neck edge, bind off 3 sts once, then 2 sts once. (23, 25, 27, 29 sts)

Dec row (WS): Work to last 3 sts, ssp-b, p1.

Rep dec row [every other row] twice more, then [every 4th row] 4 times. (16, 18, 20, 22 sts)

Work even until armhole measures same as back.

Bind off in pat.

Sleeves

With larger needles, cast on 44 (44, 46, 46) sts. Work in Seed st until sleeve measures 4 inches, ending with a WS row.

Shape cuff

Sizes extra-small and small only: K3, [k2tog, k2] 9 times, k2tog, k3. (34 sts)

Sizes medium and large only: [K4, k2tog, k3, k2tog] 2 times, [k3, k2tog] 4 times, k4. (38 sts)

All sizes: Work 1 row garter st. Change to Seed st.

Inc 1 st (M1) each end [every 6th row] 0 (0, 0, 7) times, [every 8th row] 11 (11, 10, 6) times, then [every 10th row] 0 (0, 1, 0) times. (56, 56, 60, 64 sts)

Work even until sleeve measures 20¼ (20½, 21, 20¾) inches ending with a WS row.

Bind off in pat.

Sew shoulder seams.

Neck Band

With smaller needles and RS facing, pick up and knit 59 sts evenly around neckline.

Work in garter st for 1 inch.

Bind off all sts loosley.

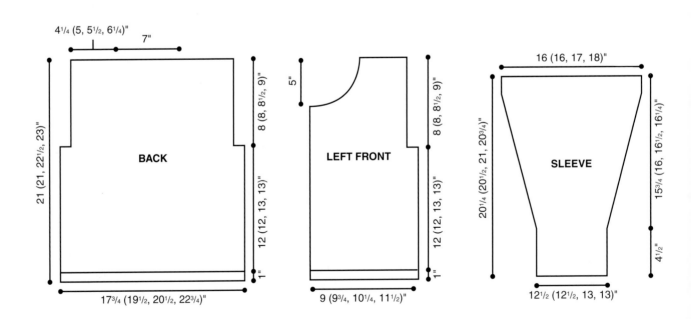

Button Band

With smaller needles and RS facing, pick up and knit 52 (52, 54, 56) sts evenly along left front edge.
Work in garter st for 1 inch.
Bind off all sts loosley.

Buttonhole Band

Work as for button band until band measures ½ inch, ending with a WS row.
Pm for button ½ inch from top of neck band.

Buttonhole row: Work to marker, bind off 2 sts, work to end of row.
On following row, cast on 2 sts over bound-off sts of previous row. Continue in garter st until band measures 1 inch from beg.
Bind off all sts loosley.

Assembly

Sew sleeves into armhole.
Sew sleeve and side seams.
Sew on button. ■

Autumn Elegance

Design by Barbara Venishnick

Looped fringe at the openings of this jacket add an element of style and elegance.

Skill Level
■■■□
INTERMEDIATE

Size
Woman's small (medium, large) Instructions are given for smallest size, with larger sizes in parentheses. When only 1 number is given, it applies to all sizes.

Finished Measurements
Chest: 40 (46, 50) inches
Length: 26¼ (26¾, 27¼) inches

Materials
• Brown Sheep Lamb's Pride Worsted, 85 percent wool/15 percent mohair worsted weight yarn (190 yds/4 oz per skein): 7 (7, 8) skeins oregano #M113 (A), 6 (7, 7) skeins wild oak #M08 (B)
• Size 11 (8mm) needles or size needed to obtain gauge
• 1 large snap set

Gauge
13 sts and 18 rows = 4 inches/10cm in pat st
To save time, take time to check gauge.

Special Abbreviation
M1 (Make 1): Make a backward lp and place on RH needle.

Pattern Stitch
Slipped Lines
Row 1 (RS): P3, *sl 1 wyif, p3; rep from * across.

Row 2: K3, *p1, k3; rep from * across.
Rep Rows 1–2 for pat.

Pattern Note
One strand each of A and B are held tog for entire garment.

Back
With 2 strands of yarn held tog, cast on 67 (75, 83) sts.
Work even in Slipped Lines pat until back measures 15 inches, ending with a WS row.
Shape underarms
Bind off at each arm edge [3 (4, 5) sts] twice, [2 (3, 4) sts] twice, [2 sts] twice, then [1 st] twice. (51, 55, 59 sts)
Work even until armhole measures 9½ (10, 10½) inches, ending with a WS row.
Shape shoulders
Bind off at each arm edge [4 sts] 8 (6, 4) times, then [0 (5, 5) sts] 0 (2, 4) times.
Place rem 19 (21, 23) sts on holder for back of neck.

Right Front
Cast on 36 (40, 44) sts.
Keeping first st of every RS row in St st for selvage, work even in Slipped Lines pat on rem sts until front measures same as for back to underarm.
Bind off at arm edge [3 (4, 5) sts] once, [2 (3, 4) sts] once, [2 sts] once, then [1 st] once. (28, 30, 32 sts)
Work even until armhole measures 5¼ inches, ending with a RS row.

Shape neck

Dec 1 st at front edge [every other row] 12 (13, 14) times. (16, 17, 18 sts)

At the same time, when armhole measures same as for back, bind off at arm edge [4 sts] 4 (3, 2) times, then [0 (5, 5) sts] 0 (1, 2) times.

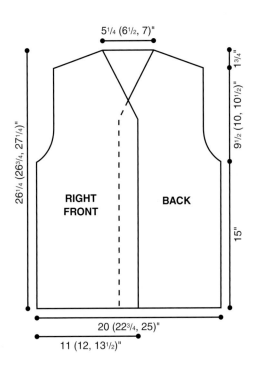

Left Front

Work as for right front, reversing shaping
Sew shoulder seams.

Sleeves

Cast on 35 (39, 43) sts.

Working in Slipped Lines pat, inc 1 st each end [every 6th row] 9 times. (53, 57, 61 sts)

Work even until sleeve measures 15 inches.

Shape sleeve cap

Bind off at arm end [3 (4, 5) sts] twice, [2 (3, 4) sts] twice, [2 sts] twice, then [1 st] twice. (37 sts)

Dec 1 st each end [every other row] 9 (10, 11) times. (19, 17, 15 sts)

Bind off 2 sts at the beg of the next 4 (4, 2) rows.

Bind off rem 11 (9, 11) sts.

Collar

With WS facing, pick up and knit 29 (28, 29) sts along shaped edge of left neck, knit across 19 (21, 23) sts of back neck, pick up and knit 29 (28, 29) sts along right neck edge. (77, 77, 81 sts)

Beg with Row 2 of Slipped Lines pat and keeping first and last st in St st, work even until collar measures 5 inches above picked-up row, ending with a WS row.

Inc row: *K1 [p1, M1] twice, p1; rep from *, end last rep k1.

Bind off purlwise on WS.

Assembly

Sew sleeves into armholes matching underarm and cap shaping.

Sew sleeve and side seams.

Fringe

With 3 strands of color A held tog, cast on 3 sts.

Row 1 (RS): K1, sl 1 wyib, k1.

Row 2: Purl.

Rep Rows 1–2 for instructed length.

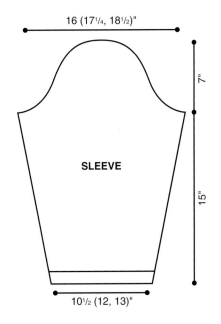

Bind off on RS row as follows: bind off 1 st, pull yarn through lp on needle. The last st will be unraveled to form lps after the fringe is sewn to the garment.

Attach fringe

Right and left front edges: Measure from lower edge to beg of neck decs. Beg at bottom and work to neck opening with RS of fringe and front next to each other, sew first st of fringe to selvage st of front.

Collar: Measure from picked-up st at neckline, around entire collar to picked-up st on opposite side. Sew in place as for fronts.

Sleeves: Make 2 strips, each 10½ (12, 13) inches long. Place first st of fringe next to cast-on edge of sleeve. Sew in place as for front. Unravel all lps.

Sew on snap.

Belt

With 1 strand each of A and B held tog, cast on 11 sts.

Every row: K1-b, k9, sl 1 wyif. Rep this row until belt measures 52 inches, or desired length. ■

Fair Isle Basket-Weave Jacket

Design by Jean Schafer-Albers

A two-color, basket-weave pattern adds a touch of spring to a go-everywhere cardigan.

Skill Level

■■■□
INTERMEDIATE

Size

Woman's small (medium, large, extra-large) Instructions are given for smallest size, with larger sizes in parentheses. When only 1 number is given, it applies to all sizes.

Finished Measurements

Chest (buttoned): 41½ (45¼, 48¾, 52½) inches
Length: 24½ (24½, 25½, 25½) inches

Materials

- Brown Sheep Nature Spun 100 percent wool worsted weight yarn (245 yds/100g per skein): 5 (5, 6, 6) skeins spring green #109 (MC), 2 (2, 3, 3) skeins snow #740 (CC)
- Size 7 (4.5mm) 29-inch circular needles or size needed to obtain gauge
- Stitch markers
- Stitch holders
- 6 (¾-inch) buttons

4 MEDIUM

Gauge

18 sts and 24 rows= 4 inches/10cm in rev St st
To save time, take time to check gauge.

Pattern Note

Selvage sts are kept in St st throughout garment.

Body

With MC, cast on 183 (199, 215, 231) sts.
Purl 1 row.
Next row (RS): K1 MC for selvage, work Row 1 of chart to last st, k1 MC for selvage.
Work even in established pat until body measures approx 15 inches, ending with Row 4 of pat.
Cut CC.
Next row (RS): Purl, dec 9 (9, 13 17) sts evenly. (174, 190, 202, 214 sts)
Knit 1 row.
Pm after sts 44 (48, 52, 55) and 130 (142, 150, 159) to denote underarm seams.

Divide for fronts and back

Next row (RS): Purl to 7 sts before underarm marker, place sts just worked on holder for right front, bind off 14 sts for right underarm, purl to 7 sts before 2nd marker, place rem sts on 2nd holder.

Back

Working on rem 72 (80, 84, 90) sts for back, dec 1 st each end [every other row] 5 (7, 8, 9) times. (62 66, 68, 72 sts)

Work even until armhole measures 9 (9, 10, 10) inches.

Place sts on 3 holders, having 16 (17, 17, 18) for each shoulder and 30 (32, 34, 36) for back neck.

Left Front

With RS facing, join yarn at back. Bind off 14 sts for underarm, work to end of row.

Dec 1 st at arm edge [every other row] 5 (7, 8, 9) times. (32, 34, 37, 39 sts)

Work even until armhole measures 6 (6, 7, 7) inches, ending with a RS row.

Shape neck

Bind off at neck edge 7 sts once, 3 sts 1 (1, 2, 2) times, then 2 sts 1 (2, 2, 2) times. (20, 20, 20, 22 sts)

Dec 1 st at neck edge [every other row] 4 (3, 3, 4) times. (16, 17, 17, 18 sts)

Work even until armhole measures same as for back.

Place all sts on holder.

Right Front

With WS facing, join yarn at underarm. Work as for left front, reversing shaping.

Join shoulders using 3-needle bind-off method.

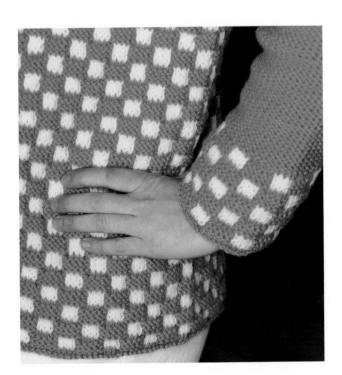

Sleeves

With MC, cast on 50 sts.

Purl 1 row.

Next row (RS): K1 MC for selvage, referring to chart, work 8-st rep 6 times, k1 MC for selvage.

Work even until 20 rows of chart have been completed.

Cut CC.

Next row (RS): K1, purl to last st dec 8 sts evenly, k1. (42 sts)

Working in rev St st, inc 1 st each end [every 6th (4th, 4th, 4th) row] 5 (15, 15, 12) times, then [every 4th (0, 2nd, 2nd) row] 7 (0, 1, 7) times. (66, 72, 74, 80 sts)

Work even until sleeve measures 15 (15¼, 15½, 15½) inches, ending with a WS row.

Shape sleeve cap

Bind off 7 sts at beg of next 2 rows. (52, 58, 60, 66 sts)

Dec 1 st each end [every other row] 5 (7, 8, 9) times, [every 4th row] 5 (4, 4, 2) times, then [every other row] 4 (5, 6, 9) times. (24, 26, 24, 26 sts)

Knit 1 row.

Bind off 2 sts at beg of next 4 rows.

Bind off rem 16 (18, 16, 18) sts.

Neck Band

With CC and RS facing, pick up and knit 21 (22, 23, 23) sts along right edge of neck, knit across 30 (32, 34, 36) sts of back neck, pick up and knit 21 (22, 23, 23) sts along left edge of neck. (72, 76, 80, 82 sts)

Work in garter st for 8 rows.

Bind off.

Button Band

With CC and RS facing, pick up and knit 3 sts for every 4 rows along left front edge.

Work in garter st for 8 rows.

Bind off.

Buttonhole Band

Pick up and knit as for button band. Knit 2 rows.

Mark band for 6 buttonholes evenly spaced,

beg and ending approx ½ inch from top and bottom.

Buttonhole row (RS): [Knit to marker, bind off 3 sts] 6 times, knit to end of row.

Next row: Knit, casting on 3 sts over previous bound-off sts.

Knit 4 more rows.

Bind off.

Assembly

Sew sleeve seams.

Sew sleeves into armholes.

Sew on buttons. ■

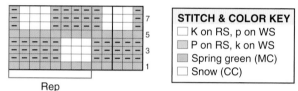

Rep

BASKET WEAVE CHART

STITCH & COLOR KEY	
☐	K on RS, p on WS
▨	P on RS, k on WS
▨	Spring green (MC)
☐	Snow (CC)

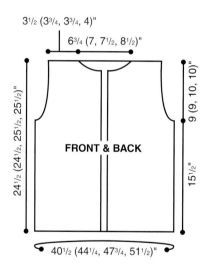

3½ (3¾, 3¾, 4)"

6¾ (7, 7½, 8½)"

9 (9, 10, 10)"

24½ (24½, 25½, 25½)"

FRONT & BACK

15½"

40½ (44¼, 47¾, 51½)"

15 (16, 16½, 17¾)"

7¼ (7½, 8½, 8½)"

22¼ (23¾, 24, 24)"

15 (15¼, 15½, 15½)"

SLEEVE

11"

Jade Stripes Jacket

Design by Cindy Polfer

This thick and warm jacket is quick to knit and fun to wear. It is knitted sideways in garter and stockinette st, and features a hidden zipper and front pockets.

Skill Level

■■■□
EXPERIENCED

Size
Woman's small (medium, large, extra-large) Instructions are given for smallest size, with larger sizes in parentheses. When only 1 number is given, it applies to all sizes.

Finished Measurements
Chest: 46 (50, 54, 58) inches
Armhole depth: 11½ (12, 12½ 12¾) inches
Sleeve length: 19 (19, 19, 19) inches
Length: 26 (26½, 27, 27½) inches

Materials
- Brown Sheep Lamb's Pride Bulky 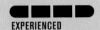 85 percent wool/15 percent mohair (125 yds/4 oz per skein): 11 (12, 13, 14) skeins jaded dreams #M190 (MC), 8 (8, 8, 9) skeins spruce #M52 (CC)
- Size 9 (5.5mm) needles
- Size 11 (8mm) needles or size needed to obtain gauge
- Stitch holders
- Stitch markers
- 24-inch separating zipper
- 1 (1⅛-inch) shank-type button
- Matching sewing thread
- Worsted weight waste yarn
- Size K/10½ (6.5mm) crochet hook

Gauge
10 sts and 18 rows = 4 inches/10cm in pat st
To save time, take time to check gauge.

Special Abbreviation and Method
M1 (Make 1): Insert LH needle under bar between sts from front to back, purl into back of this st.
Provisional Cast On: With crochet hook, very loosely ch number of sts needed for cast on. With garment yarn, pick up 1 st in each underside lp of ch. Remove cast on as directed.

Pattern Stitches
A. Stripes
Rows 1 (RS)–5: With MC, knit.
Rows 6–9: With MC, purl.
Row 10: With CC, purl.
Row 11: With CC, knit.
Rows 12 and 13: With CC, rep Rows 10 and 11.
Rows 14 and 15: With MC, purl.
Rows 16–19: With CC, rep Rows 10–13.
Rows 20–24: With MC, purl.
Rows 25–28: With MC, knit.
Row 29: With CC, knit.
Row 30: With CC, purl.
Rows 31 and 32: With CC, rep Rows 29 and 30.
Rows 33 and 34: With MC, knit.
Rows 35–38: With CC, rep Rows 29–32.
Rep Rows 1–38 for pat.

B. 1/1 Rib
Row 1 (RS): K1, *p1, k1; rep from * across.
Row 2: P1, *k1, p1; rep from * across.
Rep Rows 1 and 2 for pat.

Pattern Notes
Two strands of yarn are held tog for main garment pieces.

Single strands are used for neck, wrist and bottom bands.

Fronts are knit from center to side; back is worked from right seam to left seam.

Sleeves are knitted from armhole to wrist.

Provisional cast on is used on the back to provide open sts to be picked up for sleeves and side seam.

Garment is seamed at sides for stability, using a special technique of pulling one set of sts through another and then binding them off.

Right Front

Beg at front facing with 2 strands of CC held tog and larger needles, provisionally cast on 48 (49, 50, 51) sts.

Work in St st for 4 rows, ending with a WS row.

Marking first st of Row 1 as neck edge, work even in Stripes pat until 11 rows have been completed.

Inc 1 st at neck edge on next and [every following 3rd row] 5 times. (53, 54, 55, 56 sts)

Work even through Row 25.

Row 26: Work to end of row, cast on 7 sts. (60, 61, 62, 63 sts)

Work even for 3 rows.

Divide for pocket opening

Row 30: Work across 7 sts and place on holder; do not cut yarn.

Beg pocket lining

With smaller needles and single strand of CC, cast on 10 sts.

Using needle with cast-on sts, work [p1, M1, p1] 7 times over next 14 sts of front, place rem 39 (40, 41, 42) sts on 2nd holder. (31 sts)

Beg with a knit row, work even in St st on pocket lining sts only until lining measures 8 inches, ending with a WS row.

Next row: K21, bind off rem 10 sts. Cut yarn.

Join pocket lining

With WS facing, sl 7 sts to larger RH needle, pick up dropped yarn and work [p2tog, p1] 7 times over lining sts, purl across sts of 2nd holder. (60, 61, 62, 63 sts)

Beg with Row 31 of pat, work even for 27 (31, 36, 40) more rows, ending with Row 19 (23, 28, 32) of pat.

Cut yarn leaving a 48-inch end for sewing.

Place sts on 2 holders, 30 (31, 32, 33) for armhole and 30 for side seam.

Bottom Band

With RS facing, using smaller needles and single strand of CC, pick up and knit 55 (59, 65, 69) sts along lower edge leaving facing free.

Work even in 1/1 Rib for 6 inches.

Bind off in pat.

Left Front

With 2 strands of CC and larger needles, provisionally cast on 48 (49, 50, 51) sts.

Knit 1 row. Mark end of row as neck edge.

Beg with Row 10 of Stripes pat, work even for 2 rows.

Inc 1 st at neck edge on next and [every following 3rd row] 5 times. (53, 54, 55, 56 sts)

Work even through Row 26.

Row 27: Work to end of row, cast on 7 sts. (60, 61, 62, 63 sts)

Work even for 2 rows.

Divide for pocket opening

Row 30: Work across 39 (40, 41, 42) sts and place on holder; do not cut yarn.

Beg pocket lining

With single strand of CC and smaller needles, [p1, M1, p1] 7 times over next 14 sts of front, cast on 10 sts on end of needle, place rem 7 sts on 2nd holder. (31 sts)

Work left front and bottom band as for right, reversing shaping.

Back

With CC (MC, MC, CC) and larger needles, provisionally cast on 60 (61, 62, 63) sts.

Mark beg of cast-on row as neck edge.

Beg with Row 30 (26, 2, 36) of pat, work even for 30 (34, 39, 43) rows ending with Row 21 (21, 2, 2) of pat.

Shape back neck

Dec 1 st at neck edge [every row] 3 times. (57, 58, 59, 60 sts)

Work even for 39 rows ending with row 24 (24, 5, 5) of pat.

Inc 1 st at neck edge [every row] 3 times. (60, 61, 62, 63 sts)

Work even for 30 (34, 39, 43) rows ending with row 19 (23, 9, 13) of pat.

Divide sts placing 30 sts on 1 holder for side seam and 30 (31, 32, 33) sts on 2nd holder for armhole.

Remove sts of provisional cast on and place resulting sts on 2 holders for side seam and armhole.

Bottom Band

With RS facing, using smaller needles and single strand of CC, pick up and knit 103 (111, 121, 129) sts along bottom edge.

Work band as for fronts.

Sew shoulder seams, matching stripes.

Sleeves

Sl armhole sts from holders onto larger needle. Do not use sts involved in shoulder seam. (58, 60, 62, 64 sts)

With RS facing and 2 strands of MC (MC, CC, MC), beg sleeve with Row 1 (5, 29, 33) of pat.

Dec 1 st each end [every 5th row] 10 (7, 7, 7) times, then [every 4th row] 3 (7, 7, 7) times. (32, 32, 34, 36 sts)

Work even in established pat until sleeve measures 16 inches or desired length, dec 1 st at end of last WS row.

Beg cuff

Change to smaller needles and 1 strand of CC. Knit 1 row.

Work even in 1/1 Rib for 6 inches.

Place sts on waste yarn.

Collar

With RS facing and leaving facing sts free, using smaller needles and single strand of CC, pick

up and knit 36 sts from right front neck edge, 47 sts from back, and 28 sts from left front neck edge. (111 sts)

Work even in 1/1 Rib for 3 inches.

Bind off in pat.

Assembly

Join side seams

Sl side seam sts from holders to separate needles. Do not join yarn yet.

Hold needles parallel with RS of garment tog. With a 3rd (free) needle, sl first st of front needle knitwise, sl first st of back needle purlwise, pass first st over 2nd.

(First st of back needle is the only one now on RH needle.)

Sl next st on front needle knitwise, sl next st of back needle purlwise, pass front st over back st. (2 sts on RH needle)

Rep from * to * until all sts of back needle are on RH needle.

Turn, join matching yarn and bind off sts in usual manner.

Sew side ribbing seams. Turn up bottom band and sew in place.

Turn collar to inside and sew in place.

Sew sleeve seams.

Fold cuff to inside. Tack cuff sts to first row of ribbing, remove waste yarn.

Fold right facing to inside. Tack first row of sts to first row of pat, remove waste yarn.

Sew in zipper.

Sew edges of pocket lining tog. Fold pocket linings toward center front. Tack upper and bottom corners to garment along zipper-tape edge. Tack lower pocket edge to top of bottom rib.

Join 2 strands of MC to top of collar. With crochet hook, make a ch approx 3 inches long. Cut yarn, leaving a 6-inch end. Forming a lp, sew end to lower edge of collar. Sew on button. ■

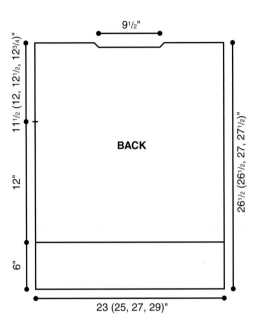

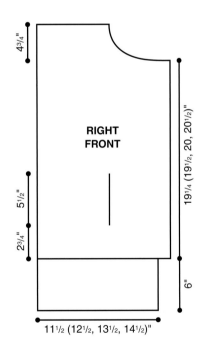

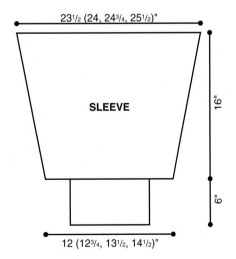

Textured Stripes

Design by Melissa Leapman

Seed stitch combines with tropical colors in an easygoing summer top.

Skill Level

EASY

Size
Woman's small (medium, large, extra-large, 2X-large) Instructions are given for smallest size, with larger sizes in parentheses. When only 1 number is given, it applies to all sizes.

Finished Measurements
Chest: 36½ (40, 46, 49) inches

Materials
• Brown Sheep Cotton Fleece 80 percent Pima cotton/20 percent Merino wool worsted weight yarn (215 yds/100g per skein): 2 (2, 3, 3, 3) skeins each coral sunset #CW225 (A) and barn red #CW201 (B), 1 (1, 2, 2, 3) skeins cavern #CW005 (C)
• Size 6 (4mm) needles or size needed to obtain gauge
• Stitch markers

Gauge
20 sts and 32 rows = 4 inches/10cm in Textured Stripes pat
To save time, take time to check gauge.

Pattern Stitch
Textured Stripes: (Uneven number of sts)
Row 1 (RS): With A, k1, *p1, k1; rep from * across.
Rows 2–8: With A, rep Row 1.
Row 9: With C, knit.
Row 10: With C, purl.

Row 11: With B, knit.
Rows 12–18: With B, rep Row 1.
Rows 19 and 20: With C, rep Rows 9 and 10.
Row 21: With A, knit.
Rep Rows 2–21 for pat.

Back
With A, cast on 91 (99, 107, 115, 123) sts. Work even in Textured Stripes pat until back measures 17 (17½, 18, 18½, 19) inches, ending with a WS row.

Shape neck

Next row: Work across 38 (42, 46, 50, 54) sts, join 2nd ball of yarn and bind off next 15 sts, work to end row.

Working on both sides of neck with separate balls of yarn, bind off at each neck edge [3 sts] once, then [2 sts] twice.

Dec 1 st each side of neck [every row] twice, then [every other row] twice. (27, 31, 35, 39, 43 sts rem each side)

Work even until back measures 19 (19½, 20, 20½, 21) inches from beg, ending with a WS row.

Shape shoulders

Bind off at each arm edge 7 (8, 9, 10, 11) sts 3 times, then 6 (7, 8, 9, 10) sts once.

Front

Work as for back.

Sleeves

With A, cast on 59 (59, 63, 65, 65) sts.
Working in Textured Stripes pat, inc 1 st each

end [every other row] 2 (6, 10, 14, 14) times, then [every 4th row] 9 (7, 4, 1, 1) times. (81, 85, 91, 95, 95 sts)

Work new sts into pat.

Work even until sleeve measures 5½ (5½, 5, 4½, 4½) inches, ending with a WS row.

Bind off all sts.

Sew left shoulder seam.

Neck Band

With RS facing and A, pick up and knit 119 sts along neckline.

Knit 1 row, purl 1 row.

Bind off.

Assembly

Sew right shoulder seam, including side of neck band.

Pm 8 (8½, 9, 9½, 9½) inches down from each shoulder seam.

Sew in sleeves between markers.

Sew sleeve and side seams. ■

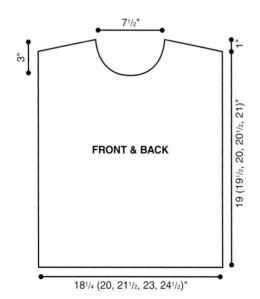

FRONT & BACK

7½"

3"

1"

19 (19½, 20, 20½, 21)"

18¼ (20, 21½, 23, 24½)"

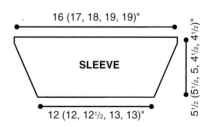

SLEEVE

16 (17, 18, 19, 19)"

12 (12, 12½, 13, 13)"

5½ (5½, 5, 4½, 4½)"

Summer Berry Shell

Design by Sandi Prosser

The lower border of this shell brings to mind luscious summer berries. Doesn't the motif remind you of a berry basket?

Skill Level
◼◼☐☐
EASY

Size
Woman's small (medium, large, extra-large) Instructions are given for smallest size, with larger sizes in parentheses. When only 1 number is given, it applies to all sizes.

Finished Measurements
Chest: 37 (40, 43½, 46½) inches
Length: 22½ (23, 24, 25) inches

Materials
- Brown Sheep Cotton Fleece 80 percent Pima cotton/20 percent Merino wool worsted weight yarn (215 yds/100g per skein): 4 (4, 5, 5) skeins berry #CW850
- Size 5 (3.75mm) needles
- Size 6 (4mm) needles or size needed to obtain gauge
- Stitch holders

Gauge
21 sts and 29 rows = 4 inches/10cm in St st with larger needles
To save time, take time to check gauge.

Back
With larger needles, cast on 98 (106, 114, 122) sts.
Work even in St st for 4 rows.
Picot turning row (RS): K1, *yo, k2tog; rep from * to last st, k1.

Work in St st for 5 rows.
Change to smaller needles.

Beg border
Row 1 (RS): K1, [yo, k2tog] 4 times, k8; rep from * to last 1 (9, 1, 9) sts, [yo, k2tog] 0 (4, 0, 4) times, k1.
Row 2 and all WS rows: Purl.
Row 3: K1, *[ssk, yo] 4 times, k8; rep from * to last 1 (9, 1, 9) sts, [ssk, yo] 0 (4, 0, 4) times, k1.
Rows 5–12: Rep Rows 1–4.
Row 13: K1, *k8, [yo, k2tog] 4 times; rep from * to last 1 (9, 1, 9) sts, k1 (9, 1, 9).
Row 15: K1, *k8, [ssk, yo] 4 times; rep from * to last 1 (9, 1, 9) sts, k1 (9, 1, 9).
Rows 17–24: Rep Rows 13–16.
Rows 25–36: Rep Rows 1–4.
Change to larger needles.
Work even in St st until back measures 14½ (15, 15½, 16) inches above picot turning row, ending with a WS row.

Shape armhole
Bind off 5 (6, 7, 7) sts at beg of next 2 rows. (88, 94, 100, 108 sts)
Dec row (RS): K2, k2tog, knit to last 4 sts, ssk, k2.
Purl 1 row.
Rep last 2 rows 5 times more. (76, 82, 88, 96 sts)
Work even until armhole measures 5½ (5½, 6, 6½) inches, ending with a WS row.

Shape neck and shoulders
K15 (17, 20, 23), sl center 46 (48, 48, 50) sts to holder, join 2nd ball of yarn and work to end of row.
Purl 1 row.

Dec row: Working on both sides of neck with separate balls of yarn, knit to last 3 sts of first side, k2tog, k1; on 2nd side, k1, ssk, knit to end of row.
Purl 1 row.
Rep last 2 rows 4 times more. (10, 12, 15, 18 sts left on each side)
Work even until armhole measures 8 (8, 8½, 9) inches.
Bind off all shoulder sts.

Front
Work as for back.
Sew front and back tog at right shoulder.

Neck Edging
With RS facing and smaller needles, pick up and knit 152 (156, 156, 160) sts evenly around neck including sts on holders.
Knit 2 rows.
Bind off all sts knitwise.
Sew left shoulder and edging seam.

Arm Edging
With RS facing and smaller needles, pick up and knit 92 (94, 98, 102) sts around armhole.
Work as for neck edging.

Assembly
Sew side seams.
Fold picot hem to inside and sew in place. ■

Silk Cabled Shell

Design by Kennita Tully

A dramatic cable and wide ribs highlight a classic shell. Wear it everywhere, from casual to elegant affairs.

Skill Level

INTERMEDIATE

Size

Woman's small (medium, large, extra-large) Instructions are given for smallest size, with larger sizes in parentheses. When only 1 number is given, it applies to all sizes.

Finished Measurements

Chest: 36 (40, 44, 48) inches
Length: 20 (21, 22, 23) inches

Materials

- Brown Sheep Prairie Silks 72 percent wool/18 percent mohair/10 percent silk worsted weight yarn (88 yds/50g per skein): 7 (8, 9, 10) skeins dough #PS100
- Size 8 (5mm) needles or size needed to obtain gauge
- Cable needle
- Stitch markers
- Size G/6 (4mm) crochet hook

4 MEDIUM

Gauge

18 sts and 20 rows = 4 inches/10cm in rib pat
To save time, take time to check gauge.

Special Abbreviations

BC (Back Cross): Sl 1 st to cn and hold in back, k2, k2 from cn.
FC (Front Cross): Sl 2 sts to cn and hold in front, k2, k2 from cn.

Pattern Stitch

Staghorn Cable (panel of 16 sts)
Rows 1, 3 and 5 (WS): Purl.
Row 2: K4, BC, FC, k4.
Row 4: K2, BC, k4, FC, k2.
Row 6: BC, k8, FC.
Rep Rows 1–6 for pat.

Pattern Notes

All decs for underarm and neck shaping are worked 1 st in from each edge.

First and last 2 sts at armhole and neck edge are kept in St st to ease later working of crochet trim.

Back

Cast on 82 (90, 98, 106) sts.

Set up pat (WS): P4, [k2, p2] 1 (2, 3, 4) times, k2, p3, k2, [p4, k2] 3 times, pm, work Staghorn Cable pat over next 16 sts, pm, [k2, p4] 3 times, k2, p3, k2, [p2, k2] 1 (2, 3, 4) times, p4.

Keeping sts between markers in Staghorn Cable pat, and rem in established rib pat, *at the same time* work side shaping by dec 1 st each end [every 4th row] 4 times. (74, 82, 94, 98 sts)

Inc 1 st each end [every 8th row] 4 times. (82, 90, 98, 106 sts)

Work even until back measures 11½ (12, 12½, 13) inches, ending with a WS row.

Shape armhole

Bind off 5 (6, 7, 8) sts at beg of next 2 rows. (72, 78, 84, 90 sts)

Dec 1 st each end [every RS row] 6 times. (60, 66, 72, 78 sts)

Work even until armhole measures 7½ (8, 8½, 9) inches, ending with a WS row.

Shoulder shaping

Bind off 5 (5, 6, 7) sts at beg of next 4 rows, then 4 (6, 6, 6) sts at beg of following 2 rows. Bind off rem 32 (34, 36, 38) sts.

Front

Work as for back until armhole measures 5½ (5¾, 6, 6½) inches, ending with a WS row.

Shape neck

Work across 22 (25, 28, 31) sts, join 2nd ball of yarn and bind off center 16 sts, work to end of row.

Working on both sides of neck with separate balls of yarn, bind off at each neck edge [2 sts] 2 (2, 3, 3) times.

Dec 1 st at each neck edge [every other row] 4 (5, 4, 5) times. (14, 16, 18, 20 sts)

At the same time, when armhole measures same as for back, work shoulder shaping as for back.

Assembly

Sew shoulder seams.
Sew side seams.

Neck Trim

Beg at center back neck and working from left to right, work 1 row sc around entire neck line. Fasten off.

Rep for armholes, beg at underarm. ■

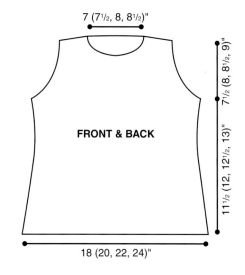

7 (7½, 8, 8½)"

7½ (8, 8½, 9)"

FRONT & BACK

11½ (12, 12½, 13)"

18 (20, 22, 24)"

My Blue Heaven

Design by Colleen Smitherman

Raglan shaping makes the most of the subtle stripes on a comfy top that will go admirably with other garments in your wardrobe.

Skill Level

▰▰▰▰
EXPERIENCED

Size

Woman's small (medium, large, extra-large) Instructions are given for smallest size, with larger sizes in parentheses. When only 1 number is given, it applies to all sizes.

Finished Measurements

Chest: 36 (40, 44, 48) inches
Length: 17½ (18½, 20¼, 21) inches

Materials

- Brown Sheep Cotton Fleece 80 percent Pima cotton/20 percent Merino wool worsted weight yarn (215 yds/100g per skein): 4 (4, 5, 5) skeins my blue heaven #CW560
- Size 3 (3.25mm) 24-inch circular needle
- Size 6 (4mm) needles or size needed to obtain gauge
- Stitch markers
- Stitch holders

Gauge

20 sts and 30 rows = 4 inches/10cm in St st with larger needles
To save time, take time to check gauge.

Special Abbreviations

Ssp: Sl 2 sts individually knitwise, return these 2 sts to LH needle in this twisted position, p2tog-tbl.

Wrap: Work to turning point, take yarn to RS of fabric, sl next st purlwise, take yarn to WS, return st to LH needle, turn.

Pattern Stitch

Refined Stripes (multiple of 6 sts + 2)
Rows 1–20: Work in St st, except for Rows 3 and 17.
Rows 3 and 17 (RS): Yo, k2tog, *k4, yo, k2tog; rep from * across.
Rows 21–40: Work in rev St st.
Rep Rows 1–40 for pat.

Pattern Notes

When working wrap and st tog, lift st onto needle so it will be on WS, then knit or purl the st and its wrap tog.

Decs and yos in each row must be paired; do not work one without the other.

Work fully fashioned armhole and sleeve dec rows as follows: On a knit row, k1, ssk, knit to last 3 sts, k2tog, k1. On a purl row, p1, p2tog, purl to last 3 sts, ssp, p1.

Back

With smaller needles, cast on 95 (105, 117, 127) sts.

Knit 10 rows. Change to larger needles.

Set up pat (RS): K2 (4, 4, 3) sts, pm, [yo, k2tog, k4] 15 (16, 18, 20) times, yo, k2tog, pm, k1 (3, 3, 2) st.

Beg with Row 4 of Refined Stripes pat, work even until back measures 11 (11½, 11¾, 12) inches, ending with a WS row.

Record last row worked.
Shape raglan armholes
Bind off 1 (0, 1, 2) st at beg of next 2 (0, 2, 2) rows. (93, 105, 115, 123 sts)
Work fully fashioned dec at beg and end of next 3 (3, 2, 2) rows, work 1 row even.
Rep these 4 (4, 3, 3) rows until 45 (45, 51, 55) sts rem, ending with a WS row.
Shape neck
Sl center 9 (15, 15, 9) sts to holder.
Working on both sides of neck with separate balls of yarn and continuing raglan decs as established, *at the same time* bind off at each neck edge 5 (3, 4, 6) sts once, then 4 (2, 2, 3) sts once (once, twice, twice).
Dec 1 st at each neck edge [every row] twice.
Bind off rem sts.

Front

Work as for back to underarm, ending with a WS row.
Shape armholes
Bind off 1 (1, 4, 5) st at beg of next 2 rows.
Work fully fashioned dec at beg and end of next 4 (4, 3, 3) rows, work 1 row even.
Rep these 5 (5, 4, 4) rows until 45 (47, 49, 51) sts rem, ending with a WS row.
Place sts on holder.

Left Sleeve

With smaller needles, cast on 71 (73, 85, 87) sts.
Knit 10 rows. Change to larger needles.
To match pat stripes, beg sleeve 30 rows below row recorded for back underarm.
Set up pat (RS): K2 (3, 3, 4), pm, work appropriate row of Refined Stripes pat over next 68 (68, 80, 80) sts, k1 (2, 2, 3).
Work in established pat, inc 1 st each

end [every 10th row] 3 times. (77, 79, 91, 93 sts)
Work even until sleeve measures 5 (5, 5½, 5½) inches, ending with a WS row.

Shape raglan sleeve

Bind off 0 (0, 4, 2) sts at beg of next 0 (0, 2, 4) rows. (77, 79, 83, 85 sts)

Work fully fashioned dec at beg and end of [every RS row] 18 (19, 20, 21) times, ending with a WS row. (41, 41, 43, 43 sts)

Shape sleeve cap

Continue raglan decs as established on right edge only 6 (6, 7, 8) times more, *at the same time* work short rows as follows:

Short row (RS): Work to last 5 (5, 5, 4) sts, wrap next st, turn, work to end of row.

Next row (RS): Work to 5 (5, 5, 4) sts before last wrapped st, wrap next st, turn, work to end of row.

Rep last row 4 (4, 5, 6) times more.

Next row (RS): Work across all sts, working wraps and sts tog as you come to them. Place rem 35 (35, 36, 35) sts on holder.

Right Sleeve

Work right sleeve as for left, reversing sleeve cap shaping by working short rows on WS rows. Sew right sleeve to corresponding front and back. Join left sleeve to front only.

Neck Band

With RS facing and smaller circular needle, knit 35 (35, 36, 35) sts of left sleeve, pm, knit first st of front, pm, knit next 43 (45, 47, 49) sts across center front neck, pm, knit last st of front, pm, knit 35 (35, 36, 35) sts of right sleeve, pick up and knit 13 (10, 12, 18) sts along right edge of back neck, knit 9 (15, 15, 9) sts of center back neck, pick up and knit 13 (10, 12, 18) sts along left edge of back neck. (150, 152, 160, 166 sts)

Rows 1, 3, 5, 7 and 9 (RS): *Knit to 3 sts before marker, k2tog, k1, sl marked st, k1, ssk; rep from * once, knit to end of row.

All WS rows: Knit.

Bind off knitwise on WS.

Assembly

Sew left sleeve to left back.
Sew sleeve and side seams. ∎

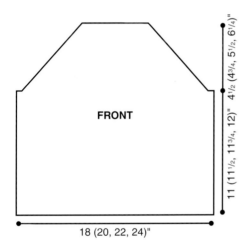

FRONT

4½ (4¾, 5½, 6¼)"

11 (11½, 11¾, 12)"

18 (20, 22, 24)"

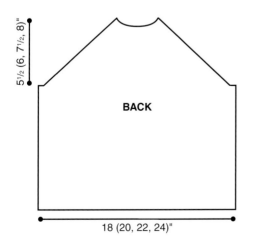

BACK

5½ (6, 7½, 8)"

18 (20, 22, 24)"

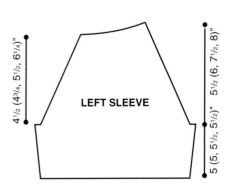

LEFT SLEEVE

4½ (4¾, 5½, 6¼)"

5½ (6, 7½, 8)"

5 (5, 5½, 5½)"

Quick Cherry Tee

Design by Melissa Leapman

Variations on a texture pattern add an attractive note to this summery top.

Skill Level

INTERMEDIATE

Size

Woman's small (medium, large, extra-large)
Instructions are given for smallest size, with larger sizes in parentheses. When only 1 number is given, it applies to all sizes.

Finished Measurements

Chest: 34 (40, 47, 53½) inches

Materials

- Brown Sheep Cotton Fleece 80 percent Pima cotton/20 percent Merino wool worsted weight yarn (215 yds/100g per skein): 5 (5, 6, 6) skeins cherry moon #CW810
- Size 5 (3.75mm) needles
- Size 6 (4mm) needles or size needed to obtain gauge

Gauge

22 sts and 30 rows = 4 inches/10cm in Garter Rib pat with larger needles
To save time, take time to check gauge.

Pattern Stitches

A. Garter Rib (multiple of 6 sts + 3)
Row 1 (RS): K3, *p3, k3; rep from * across.
Row 2: Purl.
Rep Rows 1 and 2 for pat.
B. Garter Box (multiple of 6 sts + 3)
Rows 1 and 3 (RS): Knit.
Row 2: Purl.
Rows 4, 6 and 8: K3, *p3, k3; rep from * across.

Rows 5, 7, 9 and 11: Knit.
Rows 10, 12, 14, 16 and 18: Purl.
Rows 13, 15 and 17: K3, *p3, k3; rep from * across.
Rep Rows 1–18 for pat.

Back

With larger needles, cast on 93 (111, 129, 147) sts.
Work even in Garter Rib pat until back measures 11 (11½, 12, 12½) inches, ending with a WS row.
Knit 4 rows.
Work even in Garter Box pat until back measures 14 inches, ending with a WS row.

Shape armholes

Bind off 2 (6, 6, 8) sts at beg of next 2 rows.
Dec 1 st each end [every row] 1 (6, 18, 25) times, then [every other row] 6 (6, 2, 1) times. (75, 75, 77, 79 sts)
Work even until armhole measures 6½ (7, 7½, 8) inches, ending with a WS row.

Shape neck

Work across 19 (19, 20, 21) sts, join 2nd ball of yarn and bind off next 37 sts, work to end of row.
Working on both sides of neck with separate balls of yarn, dec 1 st at each neck edge [every row] twice. (17, 17, 18, 19 sts rem each side of neck)
Work even until armhole measures 7 (7½, 8, 8½) inches, ending with a WS row.

Shape shoulders

At each arm edge bind off 4 (4, 4, 5) sts 3 times, then 5 (5, 6, 4) sts once.

Shape shoulders
At each arm edge bind off 4 (4, 4, 5) sts 3 times, then 5 (5, 6, 4) sts once.

Sleeves
With larger needles, cast on 57 sts.
Work in Garter Rib pat, inc 1 st each end [every other row] 0 (0, 3, 7) times, [every 4th row] 0 (4, 4, 2) times, then [every 6th row] 3 (1, 0, 0) times. (63, 67, 71, 75 sts)
Work added sts into pat.
Work even until sleeve measures 4 inches, ending with a WS row.

Shape sleeve cap
Bind off 2 (6, 6, 8) sts at beg of next 2 rows. (59, 55, 59, 59 sts)
Dec 1 st each end [every 4th row] 1 (5, 5, 6)

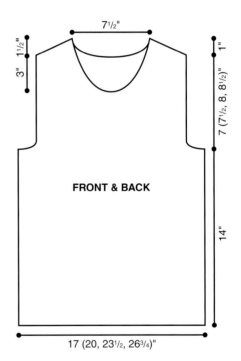

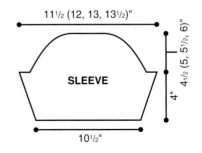

Front
Work as for back until armhole measures 3½ (4, 4½, 5) inches, ending with a WS row.
Shape neck
Work across 29 (29, 30, 31) sts, join 2nd ball of yarn and bind off next 17 sts, work to end of row.
Working on both sides of neck with separate balls of yarn, bind off at each neck edge [4 sts] once, [3 sts] once, then [2 sts] once.
Dec 1 st each side of neck [every row] 3 times. (17, 17, 18, 19 sts rem each side)
Work even until armhole measures same as for back.

times, then [every other row] 12 (6, 8, 7) times. (33 sts)
Bind off 3 sts at beg of next 4 rows.
Bind off rem 21 sts.
Sew left shoulder seam.

Neck Band

With RS facing and smaller needles, pick up and knit 116 sts along neckline.
Work in garter st for ½ inch, ending with a WS row.
Next row: Knit, dec 12 sts evenly across row. (104 sts)
Work even in garter st until band measures 1 inch.
Bind off.

Assembly

Sew right shoulder seam, including side of neck band.
Sew sleeves into armholes.
Sew sleeve and side seams. ■

Coral Lace Shell

Design by Sandi Prosser

Delicate openwork flanks fundamental cables on the front and collar of a cool summer shell.

Skill Level
■■□□
EASY

Size
Woman's extra-small (small, medium, large, extra-large) Instructions are given for smallest size, with larger sizes in parentheses. When only 1 number is given, it applies to all sizes.

Finished Measurements
Chest: 33 (35, 37, 39, 41) inches
Length: 19½ (20, 20½, 21, 22) inches

Materials
- Brown Sheep Cotton Fleece 80 percent Pima cotton/20 percent Merino wool worsted weight yarn (215 yds/100g per skein): 3 (3, 4, 4, 4) skeins coral sunset #CW225
- Size 4 (3.5mm) needles
- Size 5 (3.75mm) needles or size needed to obtain gauge
- Stitch holders
- Cable needle

3 LIGHT

Gauge
22 sts and 30 rows = 4 inches/10cm in St st with larger needles
To save time, take time to check gauge.

Special Abbreviation
C4F (Cable 4 Front): Sl 2 sts to cn and hold in front, k2, k2 from cn.

Pattern Stitches
A. Cable & Lace Panel (panel of 22 sts)
Row 1 (RS): [K2tog, yo, p2, k4, p2] twice, k2tog, yo.
Row 2 and all WS rows: [P2, k2, p4, k2] twice, p2.
Row 3: [Yo, ssk, p2, C4F, p2] twice, yo, ssk.
Row 5: Rep Row 1.
Row 7: [Yo, ssk, p2, k4, p2] twice, yo, ssk.
Row 8: Rep Row 2.
Rep Rows 1–8 for pat.

B. Open Cable
Row 1 and all WS rows: *P4, k2, p2, k2; rep from * across.
Rows 2 and 6: *P2, k2tog, yo, p2, k4; rep from * across.
Row 4: *P2, yo, ssk, p2, C4F; rep from * across.
Row 8: *P2, yo, ssk, p2, k4; rep from * across.
Rep Rows 1–8 for pat.

Back
With smaller needles, cast on 91 (95, 101, 109, 117) sts.
Row 1 (WS): Knit.
Row 2: K1, *yo, k2tog; rep from * across.
Row 3: Knit.
Change to larger needles and St st.
Work even until back measures 3 inches, ending with a WS row.
Dec row: K2, k2tog, knit to last 4 sts, ssk, k2.
Work even for 5 rows.
[Rep last 6 rows] twice. (85, 89, 95, 103, 111 sts)
Work even until back measures 8 inches, ending with a WS row.

Inc row: K1, inc 1 st in next st, knit to last 3 sts, inc 1 st in next st, k2.

Work even for 7 rows.

[Rep last 8 rows] twice. (91, 95, 101, 109, 117 sts)

Work even until back measures 12½ (12½, 13, 13, 13½) inches, ending with a WS row.

Armhole shaping

Next 2 rows: Bind off 6 sts, work to end of row. (79, 83, 89, 97,105 sts)

Row 3: K2, k2tog, knit to last 4 sts, ssk, k2.

Row 4: Purl.

[Rep Rows 3 and 4] 4 (4, 5, 5, 6) times more. (69, 73, 77, 85, 91 sts)

Next row (RS): Rep Row 3.

Work even in St st for 3 rows.

[Rep last 4 rows] 3 (3, 3, 4, 4) times more. (61, 65, 69, 75, 81 sts)

Work even until armhole measures 6½ (7, 7, 7½, 8) inches, ending with a WS row.

Shoulder and back neck shaping

Next row (RS): K11 (13, 15, 18, 21), k2tog, turn, p2tog, purl to end of row.

Row 3: Bind off 6 (7, 8, 9, 11) sts, knit to end of row.

Row 4: Purl.

Bind off rem 5 (6, 7, 9, 10) sts.

With RS facing, sl next 35 sts to holder. Rejoin yarn at next st.

Next row (RS): Ssk, knit to end of row.

Row 2: Bind off 6 (7, 8, 9, 11) sts, purl to last 2 sts, p2tog-tbl.

Row 3: Knit.

Bind off rem 5 (6, 7, 9, 10) sts.

Front

With smaller needles, cast on 91 (95, 101, 109, 117) sts.

Work first 3 rows as for back.

Next row (RS): K36 (38, 41, 45, 49), [inc 1 st in next st, k3] 5 times, k35 (37, 40, 44, 48). (96, 100, 106, 114, 122 sts)

Change to larger needles.

Set up pat: P36 (38, 41, 45, 49), k1, pm, work Row 2 of Cable & Lace panel over next 22 sts, pm, k1, p36 (38, 41, 45, 49).

Row 2: K36 (38, 41, 45, 49), p1, work Row 1 of panel, p1, k36 (38, 41, 45, 49).

Row 3: P36 (38, 41, 45, 49), k1, work Row 2 of panel, k1, p36 (38, 41, 45, 49).

Beg with Row 3 of panel, keeping sts between markers in panel pat and rem sts in St st, work side and armhole shaping as for back. (66, 70, 74, 80, 86 sts)

Work even until armhole measures 4 (4½, 4½, 5, 5½) inches, ending with a WS row.

Neck shaping

Next row: Work in pat across 20 (22, 24, 27, 30) sts, sl rem sts to holder.

Dec 1 st at neck edge [every row] 5 times, then [every other row] 4 times. (11, 13, 15, 18, 21 sts)

Work even until armhole measures same as for back.

Shoulder shaping

Bind off 6 (7, 8, 9, 11) sts at beg of next row.

Work 1 row even.

Bind off rem 5 (6, 7, 9, 10) sts.

With RS facing, sl center 26 sts to holder. Join yarn at next st.

Work 1 row in pat on rem 20 (22, 24, 27, 30) sts.

Dec 1 st at neck edge [every row]
5 times, then [every other row]
4 times. (11, 13, 15, 18, 21 sts)
Work even until armhole measures
same as for back.
Shape shoulders as for back.
Sew right shoulder seam.

Collar

With larger needles and RS facing,
pick up and knit 21 sts along left
front neck edge, work in pat across
26 sts on front neck holder, pick
up and knit 21 sts along right front
neck edge, 3 sts along right back
neck edge, knit 35 sts from back
neck holder inc 3 sts evenly, pick up
and knit 3 sts along left back neck
edge. (112 sts)
Next row: K1, *p4, k2, p2, k2; rep
from * to last st, k1.
Keeping first and last st in garter st
for selvage, and appropriate row
of Open Cable pat to match established center panel, work even until
collar measures 3 inches, ending
with a WS row.
Change to smaller needles.
Next row: Knit, dec 10 sts evenly.
(102 sts)
Knit 2 rows.
Bind off knitwise on WS.
Sew left shoulder and collar seam.

Armbands

With smaller needles and RS facing,
pick up and knit 78 (78, 82, 82, 86)
sts around armhole.
Knit 2 rows.
Bind off knitwise on WS.
Sew side seams. ▨

Summer Confection

Design by Sandi Prosser

The pastel colors in this easy sleeveless pullover are reminiscent of refreshing ice cream treats.

Skill Level

◼◼◻◻ EASY

Size

Woman's extra-small (small, medium, large, extra-large) Instructions are given for smallest size, with larger sizes in parentheses. When only 1 number is given, it applies to all sizes.

Finished Measurements

Chest: 34 (36, 38, 40, 42) inches
Length: 21½ (22, 22, 22½, 23) inches

Materials

- Brown Sheep Cotton Fleece 80 percent Pima cotton/20 percent Merino wool worsted weight yarn (215 yds/100g per skein): 2 skeins pink diamond #CW222 (A), 1 (1, 2, 2, 2) skeins cotton ball #CW100 (B), 1 (1, 1, 2, 2) skeins spryte #CW640 (C)
- Size 5 (3.75mm) needles or size needed to obtain gauge

Gauge

22 sts and 30 rows = 4 inches/10cm in St st
To save time, take time to check gauge.

Special Abbreviation

M1 (Make 1): Make a backward lp and place on RH needle.

Pattern Stitch

Stripe Pattern

Work in St st and color sequence of 7 rows each A, B and C.

Pattern Note

Carry color not in use loosely up side edge; do not cut yarn at each color change.

Back

With A, cast on 94 (100, 106, 110, 116) sts.
Beg with a knit row, work in St st for 5 rows.
Next row (WS): Knit, forming fold line.
Beg with a knit row and A, work even in Stripe Pat until back measures 3 inches above fold line, ending with a WS row.
Dec row: K2, k2tog, knit to last 4 sts, ssk, k2.
Work even for 7 rows.
[Rep last 8 rows] twice. (88, 94, 100, 104, 110 sts)
Work even until back measures 8 inches above fold line, ending with a WS row.
Inc row: K2, M1, knit to last 2 sts, M1, k2.
Work even for 9 rows.
[Rep last 10 rows] twice. (94, 100, 106, 110, 116 sts)
Work even in established color pat until back measures 14 inches above fold line, ending with a RS row.

Armhole shaping

Next 2 rows: Bind off 4 (4, 4, 5, 5) sts, work to end of row. (86, 92, 98, 100, 106 sts)
Row 3: K1, k2tog, knit to last 3 sts, ssk, k1.
Row 4: P1, p2tog-tbl, purl to last 3 sts, p2tog, p1.
Rep Rows 3 (3, 3-4-3, 3-4-3, 3-4-3).
Purl 1 row.
[Rep Row 3. Purl 1 row] 4 times. (72, 28, 80, 82, 88 sts)
Work even in established color pat until armhole measures 7 (7½, 7½, 8, 8½) inches, ending with a RS row.

Knit 4 rows.
Bind off all sts knitwise on WS.

Front
Work as for back.

Assembly
Sew shoulder seams, leaving center 10 inches on front and back open for neck.

Armbands
With A, pick up and knit 79 (83, 83, 85, 87) sts evenly around armhole edge.
Knit 2 rows.
Bind off knitwise on WS.

Finishing
Sew side seams.
Turn hem to inside and sew in place. ■

Slipped-Stitch Casual Pullover

Design by Scarlet Taylor

With its easily remembered stitch pattern and interesting texture, this casual pullover is a fun exercise in color knitting.

Skill Level

EASY

Size
Woman's small (medium, large, extra-large) Instructions are given for smallest size, with larger sizes in parentheses. When only 1 number is given, it applies to all sizes.

Finished Measurements
Chest: 36 (39, 42, 46) inches
Length: 21 (22, 23, 23) inches

Materials
- Brown Sheep Cotton Fleece 80 percent Pima cotton/20 percent Merino wool worsted weight yarn (215 yds/100g per skein): 3 (3, 4, 4) skeins each lime light #CW840 (A) and Malibu blue #CW570 (B)
- Size 4 (3.5 mm) needles
- Size 6 (4mm) needles or size needed to obtain gauge
- Stitch holder

3 LIGHT

Gauge
22 sts and 40 rows = 4 inches/10cm in Semi-Woven Tweed pat with larger needles To save time, take time to check gauge.

Special Abbreviation
M1 (Make 1): Insert LH needle under horizontal thread between st just worked and next st, knit into back of st.

Pattern Stitch
Semi-Woven Tweed
Row 1 (RS): With B, k1, *sl 1 wyib, k1; rep from * across.
Row 2: With B, purl.
Row 3: With A, k1, *sl 1 wyif, k1; rep from * across.
Row 4: With A, purl.
Row 5: With B, k2, *sl 1 wyib, k1; rep from * across, end k1.
Row 6: With B, purl.
Row 7: With A, k2, *sl 1 wyif, k1; rep from * across, end k1.
Row 8: With A, purl.
Rep Rows 1–8 for pat.

Pattern Note
All sleeve inc are worked as M1.

Back
With smaller needles and A, cast on 101 (109, 117, 129) sts.
Change to B and work in k1, p1 rib for 1½ inches, ending with a RS row.

Change to A and larger needles.
Purl 1 row.
Work even in Semi-Woven Tweed pat until back measures, 11¾ (12¼, 12¾, 12¼) inches, ending with a WS row.

Shape armholes

Next 2 rows: Bind off 5 (5, 6, 8) sts, work to end of row. (91, 99, 105, 113 sts)
Work even until armhole measures 8½ (9, 9½, 10) inches, ending with a WS row.

Shape neck

Next row (RS): Work across 30 (34, 37, 41) sts, join 2nd ball of yarn and bind off next 31 sts, work to end of row.
Working on both sides of neck with separate balls of yarn, bind off 2 sts at each neck edge. Dec 1 st at each neck edge [every other row] 3 times. (25, 29, 32, 36 sts)
Bind off rem sts.

Front

Work as for back until armhole measures 6¼ (6¾, 7¼, 7¾) inches, ending with a WS row.

Shape neck

Next row (RS): Work across 35 (39, 42, 46) sts, sl next 21 sts to holder for front neck, join 2nd ball of yarn, and work to end of row.

Working on both sides of neck with separate balls of yarn, dec 1 st at each neck edge [every other row] 10 times. (25, 29, 32, 36 sts)
Work even until armhole measures same as for back.
Bind off all sts.

Sleeves

With A and smaller needles, cast on 59 (65, 67, 75) sts.
Change to B and work in k1, p1 rib for 1½ inches, ending with a RS row.
Change to larger needles and A.
Purl 1 row.
Working in Semi-Woven Tweed pat, inc 1 st each end [every other row] 16 (16, 18, 16) times, then [every 4th row] 2 (2, 1, 2) times. (95, 101, 105, 111 sts)
Work even until sleeve measures 6 inches, ending with a WS row.
Bind off all sts.
Sew left shoulder seam.

Neck Band

With RS facing, using B and smaller needles, pick up and knit 82 sts (including sts on holder) around neckline.
Work even in k1, p1 rib for 1½ inches.
Change to A and bind off loosely in rib.

Assembly

Sew right shoulder and neck-band seam.
Sew in sleeves.
Sew sleeve and side seams. ∎

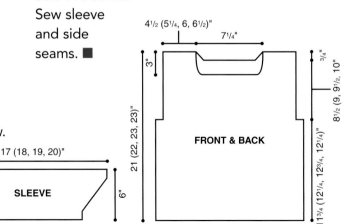

Fun in the Sun

Design by Lois S. Young

Vertical stripes add a youthful look to a tank top just meant for a fun summer day.

Skill Level

■■■□
INTERMEDIATE

Size

Woman's small (medium, large) Instructions are given for smallest size, with larger sizes in parentheses. When only 1 number is given, it applies to all sizes.

Finished Measurements

Chest: 31 (36½, 43) inches
Length: 17 (18½, 20) inches

Materials

- Brown Sheep Cotton Fleece 80 percent Pima cotton/20 percent Merino wool worsted weight yarn (215 yds/100g per skein): 2 skeins raging purple #CW730 (MC), 1 (1, 2) skeins cotton ball # CW100 (A)
- Brown Sheep Cotton Fine 80 percent Pima cotton/20 percent Merino wool sport weight yarn (222 yds/50g per skein): 1 (1, 2) skeins each cotton ball #CW100, my blue heaven #CW560, raging purple #CW730
- Size 8 (5mm) double-pointed (2 only) and straight needles or size needed to obtain gauge
- 3 (⁹⁄₁₆-inch) buttons, La Mode #4521

Gauge

20 sts and 32 rows = 4 inches/10cm in Stripe pat
To save time, take time to check gauge.

Pattern Stitch

Stripe Sequence
Rows 1, 3 and 5 (RS): With B, knit.
Rows 2, 4 and 6: With B, purl.
Rows 7–10: With MC, knit.
Rows 11 and 13: With A, knit.
Rows 12 and 14: With A, purl.
Rows 15–18: With MC, knit.
Rep Rows 1–18 for pat.

Pattern Notes

Color B is comprised of 1 strand each color of Cotton Fine held tog.

Pat is worked sideways from seam to seam and stretches slightly. Take this into consideration when choosing size.

Ratios for picking up sts for I-cord Borders are 2 sts for every 4 rows on MC stripes, 3 sts for every 4 rows on A stripes, and 4 sts for every 6 rows on B stripes.

On curves at neck and underarms, work at rate of [pick up and knit 1 st, skip 1 st] 5 times.

Beg armhole and bottom borders at side seam, neck border at right shoulder seam.

Back

With B and straight needles, cast on 44 (49, 54) sts.

Beg with Row 1 (9, 15) of Stripe pat, work even for 8 (10, 12) rows, ending with Row 8 (18, 8) of pat.

Shape armhole

Inc 1 st [at end of every RS row] 5 times, end with Row 18 (10, 18) of pat. (45, 54, 59 sts)

Beg shoulder strap
Next row (RS): Work across row, cast on 32 (34, 37) sts. (81, 88, 96 sts)
Work even for 22 (30, 30) rows, end with Row 5 (5, 13) of pat.
Next row (WS): Bind off 16 (18, 21) sts, work to end of row. (65, 70, 75 sts)
Beg neck shaping
Dec 1 st [at end of every RS row] 5 times. (60, 65, 70 sts)
Work even for 38 (38, 40) rows, end with Row 8 (8, 18) of pat.
Inc 1 st [at end of every RS row] 5 times, end with Row 18 (18, 10) of pat. (65, 70, 75 sts)
Begin second shoulder strap
Next row (RS): Work across row, cast on 16 (18, 21) sts. (81, 88, 96 sts)
Work even for 22 (30, 30) rows, end with Row 5 (13, 5) of pat.
Next row (WS): Bind off 32 (34, 37) sts, work to end of row. (49, 54, 59 sts)
Shape armhole and underarm
Dec 1 st [at end of every RS row] 5 times, end with row 16 (6, 16). (44, 49, 54 sts)
Work even for 8 (10, 12) rows.
Bind off all sts.

Front
Work as for back.

Assembly
Sew shoulder and side seams.

I-cord Borders
Beg as noted with RS facing, using MC and dpn, cast on 3 sts, pick up and knit 1 st from edge of garment.
All rows: *Slide sts to other end of needle, bring yarn around back of work to create a tube, k2, ssk, pick up and knit next st from edge of garment. Rep from * until entire opening is worked.
Sew final sts to cast-on edge of border.
Sew buttons to center front stripe, starting ½ inch below border. ■

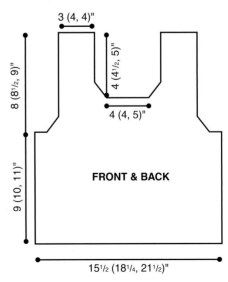

3 (4, 4)"

4 (4½, 5)"

4 (4, 5)"

8 (8½, 9)"

9 (10, 11)"

FRONT & BACK

15½ (18¼, 21½)"

Texture Time

Designs by Laura Andersson

A self-fringing scarf and a matching hat are ideal projects for the novice knitter.

Skill Level

Scarf:

BEGINNER

Hat:

EASY

Size

Hat: Adult small (medium, large) Instructions are given for smallest size, with larger sizes in parentheses. When only 1 number is given, it applies to all sizes.
Scarf: One size fits most

Finished Measurements

Hat circumference: 28 (20, 22) inches
Scarf: Approx 4 x 51 inches without fringe

Materials

- Brown Sheep Handpaint Originals 70 percent mohair/30 percent wool worsted weight yarn (88 yds/50g per hank): 4 hanks mountain majesty #HP100 (A)
- Brown Sheep Nature Spun Worsted 100 percent wool worsted weight yarn (245 yds/100g per skein): 3 skeins butterfly blue #N59 (B)
- Size 11 (8mm) 16- and 24-inch circular needles or size needed to obtain gauge

Gauge

11 sts and 16 rows = 4 inches/10cm in St st
To save time, take time to check gauge.

Pattern Stitch

Texture Time (multiple of 5 sts)
Rnd 1: *K1, p4; rep from * around.
Rnd 2: *K2, p3; rep from * around.
Rnd 3: *K3, p2; rep from * around.
Rnd 4: *K4, p1; rep from * around.
Rnd 5: Knit.
Rnd 6: Purl.
Rep Rnds 1–6 for pat.

Pattern Notes

One strand of A and 2 of B are held tog for entire hat and scarf.

Scarf is worked across the width; long strands are left at either end to form the fringe.

Hat

With 3 strands of yarn held tog, cast on 50 (55, 60) sts.

Join without twisting, pm between first and last st.

Knit 10 rnds.

Work 12 rnds of Texture Time pat.

Work even in St st until hat measures 5½ (6, 6½) inches.

Shape top

Rnd 1: *K3, k2tog; rep from * around. (40, 44, 48 sts)

Knit 1 rnd.

Rnd 3: *K2, k2tog; rep from * around. (30, 33, 36 sts)

Knit 1 rnd.

Rnd 5: *K1, k2tog; rep from * around. (20, 22, 24 sts)

Rnd 6: Rep Rnd 5, ending with k2 on small size, (k1 on medium size, k2tog on large size). (14, 15, 16 sts)

Rnd 7: K2tog around. (7, 8, 8 sts)

Cut yarn leaving a 12-inch end. Draw yarn through rem sts twice and pull tightly.

Scarf

With 3 strands of yarn held tog, cast on 175 sts, leaving a 10-inch tail at beg of row for fringe. Work Rnd 1 of Texture Time pat. Cut yarn leaving a 10-inch tail at end of row. Slide sts to opposite end of needle.

Leaving a 10-inch tail at beg and end of each row, and sliding sts to opposite end of needle before beg each new row, continue in pat for 17 more rows (3 reps of pat).

Bind off loosely.

Finishing

Make an overhand knot with tails, using 6 strands of yarn for each knot.

Trim fringe evenly. ■

Lovely Evening Scarf

Design by Nazanin S. Fard

This attractive scarf is worked in eye-pleasing stripes, which follow its triangular shape. An added bonus is that as the work progresses, the number of stitches reduces.

Skill Level
◼◼◻◻
EASY

Size
One size fits most

Finished Measurements
Top edge: 50 inches
Sides: 40 inches

Materials
- Brown Sheep Wildfoote Luxury Sock Yarn 75 percent washable wool/25 percent nylon sock yarn (215 yds/50g per ball): 1 ball each camel #SY11 (A), Zane Grey #SY36 (B), gunsmoke #SY40 (C)
- Size 7 (4.5mm) needles
- Size F/5 (3.75mm) crochet hook
- Stitch markers
- Small amount waste yarn

1 SUPER FINE

Gauge
15 sts and 38 rows = 4 inches/10cm in garter st
To save time, take time to check gauge.

Pattern Note
Carry colors not in use up side of work; do not cut yarn after each color change.

Scarf
With crochet hook and waste yarn, loosely ch 251 sts.
Turn ch over and with A pick up and knit 1 st in each bump of ch.
Row 1: K125, pm, k1, pm, k125.
Row 2: K1, ssk, knit to 2 sts before marker, ssk, k1, k2tog, knit to last 3 sts, k2tog, k1. (247 sts) Change to B.
Row 3: Knit.
Rep Rows 2 and 3, alternating colors after every 2 rows until there are 9 sts left on needle.
Next row: K1, ssk, k3, k2tog, k1. (7 sts)
Row 2: K1, ssk, k1, k2tog, k1. (5 sts)
Row 3: K1, sl 1, k2tog, psso, k1. (3 sts)
Bind off.

Border
Remove provisional cast on and place resulting lps on needle. (250 sts)
Join C.
Row 1: Knit.
Row 2: K5, *yo, k5; rep from * across. (299 sts)
Rows 3, 5, 7 and 9: Knit.
Row 4: K5, *yo, k1, yo, k5; rep from * across. (397 sts)
Row 6: K3, *k2tog, yo, k3, yo, ssk, k1; rep from *, end last rep k3.
Row 8: K2, k2tog, *yo, k5, yo, sl 1, k2tog, psso; rep from *, end last rep yo, ssk, k2.
Row 10: *Insert crochet hook into next 3 sts, pull yarn through all lps on hook, ch 5; rep from *, end last with insert hook into last 4 sts, pull yarn through all lps on hook. Leave last lp on hook.
Work 1 row of sc along the top edge.
Fasten off. ◼

October's Glory

Designs by Diane Elliott

The rich shades of fall's splendid foliage are captured in a warm, diagonal-striped scarf and matching snug beret.

Skill Level

EASY

Size
One size fits most

Finished Measurements
Scarf: Approx 5 x 60 inches
Hat circumference: 19 inches

Materials
- Brown Sheep Handpaint Originals 70 percent mohair/30 percent wool worsted weight yarn (88 yds/50g per hank): 2 hanks each New England fall #HP80 (MC) and chestnut #HP35 (CC)
- Size 6 (4mm) needles
- Size 10½ (6.5mm) needles or size needed to obtain gauge
- Stitch markers

Gauge
13 sts and 20 rows = 4 inches/10cm in St st with larger needles
To save time, take time to check gauge.

Pattern Stitch
1/1 Ribbing
Row 1 (RS): K1, *p1, k1; rep from * across.
Row 2: P1, *k1, p1; rep from * across.
Rep Rows 1 and 2 for pat.

Pattern Notes
Work pat inc by knitting in top of st in row below.
Carry yarn not in use up side of work; do not cut yarn after color change.

Scarf

With MC and larger needles, cast on 23 sts.
Foundation row (WS): K1, *p1, k1; rep from * across.
Rows 1, 3 and 5: With MC, k1, inc in next st, knit to last 3 sts, k2tog, k1.
Rows 2, 4 and 6: With MC, k1 *p1, k1; rep from * across.
Rows 7 and 9: With CC, rep Row 1.
Rows 8 and 10: With CC, rep Row 2.
Rep Rows 1–10 until scarf measures approx 60 inches, ending with Row 6 of pat.
Next row: K1, *p1, k1; rep from * across.
Bind off.

Hat

With CC and smaller needles, cast on 100 sts.
Work even in 1/1 Ribbing for 1¼ inches, inc 9 sts evenly on last WS row. (109 sts)
Rows 1, 3 and 5 (RS): With MC, k1, inc in next st, k50, k2tog, pm, k1, inc in next, k50, k2tog, k1.
Rows 2, 4 and 6: With MC, k1 *p1, k1; rep from * across.
Rows 7 and 9: With CC, rep Row 1.
Rows 8 and 10: With CC, rep Row 2.
[Work Rows 1–10] twice, rep Rows 1–4.
Shape top
Row 1: With MC, *k1, inc in next st, [k8, k2tog] 5 times, k2tog; rep from * once, k1. (99 sts)
Row 2: With MC, k1 *p1, k1; rep from * across.
Row 3: With CC, *k1, inc in next st, [k7, k2tog] 5 times, k2tog, rep from * once, k1. (89 sts)
Rows 4 and 6: With CC, rep Row 2.
Row 5: *K1, inc in next st [k6, k2tog] 5 times, k2tog, rep from * once, k1. (79 sts)

Row 7: *K2tog, k1; rep from * to last 4 sts, [k2tog] twice. (52 sts)
Row 8: Purl.
Row 9: K2tog across. (26 sts)
Row 10: P2tog across. (13 sts)

Finishing

Cut yarn, leaving a 24-inch end. Draw yarn through rem sts twice and pull tightly to close opening.
Sew seam. ∎

Jaunty Stripes Hat & Scarf

Designs by Diane Zangl

This is a beginner project, but by no means is it a beginner in the style department. The envelope hat has jaunty tassels at each corner; the scarf is worked lengthwise to accent the stripe pattern.

Skill Level

BEGINNER

Size

Adult (one size fits most)

Finished Measurements

Scarf: Approx 6½ x 60 inches
Hat circumference: 21 inches

Materials

- Brown Sheep Lamb's Pride Bulky 85 percent wool/15 percent mohair bulky weight yarn (125 yds/4 oz per skein): 3 skeins sandy heather #M01 (MC), 2 skeins white frost #M11 (CC)
- Size 9 (5.5mm) straight and 16-inch circular needles
- Size 10 (6mm) needles or size needed to obtain gauge
- 5-inch piece of cardboard

Gauge

13 sts and 20 rows = 4 inches/10cm in Ridges pat
To save time, take time to check gauge.

Pattern Stitch

Ridges
Rows 1 (WS)–3: With MC, knit.

Rows 4 and 6: With CC, knit.
Rows 5 and 7: With CC, purl.
Row 8: With MC, knit.
Rep Rows 1–8 for pat.

Pattern Note

Do not cut yarn when changing colors. Carry yarn not in use up side of work.

Scarf

With MC and larger needles, cast on 188 sts.
Work even in Ridges pat for 35 rows.
Bind off knitwise with CC.

End bands

With MC and smaller needles, RS
facing, pick up and knit 3 sts for every
4 rows along 1 short end of scarf. You must
have an uneven number of sts.

Row 1 (WS): Sl1p wyif, *k1, p1; rep from
* across.
Row 2: Sl1k wyib, *p1, k1; rep from * across.
Rep Rows 1 and 2 once.
Bind off in pat.
Rep for other end of scarf.

Hat

With MC and larger needles, cast on 26 sts.
Work even in Ridges pat until hat measures
approx 22 inches, ending with Row 7 of pat.
Bind off knitwise with CC.

Finishing

Sew bound-off edge to cast-on edge.
Matching stripes, fold hat in half. Sew top
edges tog.

Head band

With MC and smaller circular needle, pick up
and knit 3 sts for every 4 rows along lower edge
of hat, being sure to have an even number of
sts. Place marker between first and last st.
Ribbing rnd: *K1, p1; rep from * around.
Rep Ribbing rnd until band measures 1½ inches.
Bind off in pat.

Tassels (make 2)

Cut 2 strands of MC, each 8 inches long, and
set aside.
Wind CC around cardboard 15 times.
Using a reserved strand, tie 1 end; cut opposite
end.
Wrap 2nd strand around tassel, about 1 inch
below fold.
Tie tightly and hide ends in tassel.
Trim ends evenly. Attach 1 tassel to each
point of hat. ■

Checkered Denim Scarf

Design by Colleen Smitherman

This scarf is perfect for cold and windy days. The ribbed center cuddles around your neck while the ends lie flat under your coat.

Skill Level

BEGINNER

Size
One size fits most

Finished Measurements
Length: 48 inches
End width: 4½ inches
Neck width: 3 inches

Materials
- Brown Sheep Lamb's Pride Superwash Worsted 100 percent wool worsted weight yarn (200 yds/ 100g per ball): 2 balls stonewashed denim #SW150
- Size 6 (4mm) needles or size needed to obtain gauge

4 MEDIUM

Gauge
29 sts and 32 rows = 4 inches/10cm in Checkerboard pat
To save time, take time to check gauge.

Pattern Stitch
Checkerboard
Rows 1, 3, 5 and 7 (RS): K6, *p6, k6; rep from * across.
Rows 2, 4, 6 and 8: P6, *k6, p6; rep from * across.
Rows 9, 11, 13 and 15: Rep Row 2.
Rows 10, 12, 14 and 16: Rep Row 1.
Rep Rows 1–16 for pat.

Scarf
Cast on 30 sts.
[Rep Rows 1–16 of Checkerboard pat] 7 times.
Begin ribbed section
Row 1 (RS): K2, *p2, k2; rep from * across.
Row 2: P2, *k2, p2; rep from * across.
Rep Rows 1 and 2 until ribbed section measures 22 inches.
Begin checkerboard section
[Rep Rows 1–16 of Checkerboard pat] 7 times. Bind off.

Finishing
Block scarf, flattening checkerboard sections and expanding ribbed section as desired. ■

Bubblegum Hat & Wristers

Designs by Diane Zangl

Fun yarn, bright colors—from preteen to adult, who wouldn't enjoy these colorful accessories?

Skill Level

EASY

Size

Teen (adult) Instructions are given for smaller size, with larger size in parentheses. When only 1 number is given, it applies to both sizes.

Finished Measurements

Hat circumference: 20 (22) inches
Wristers: 8 (9) inches long

Materials

- Brown Sheep Waverly Woolcolors 100 percent wool worsted weight yarn (solids: 162 yds/4 oz per hank; handpaint: 81 yds/2 oz per hank): 4 hanks peach/blue/white #8900 (MC), 1 hank peach #3094 (CC)
- Size 5 (3.75mm) double-pointed and 16-inch circular needles
- Size 7 (4.5mm) double-pointed and 16-inch circular needles or size needed to obtain gauge
- Stitch markers
- 5-inch piece of cardboard

Gauge

16 sts and 22 rows = 4 inches/10cm in rev St st
To save time, take time to check gauge.

Hat

With CC and smaller circular needle, cast on 80 (88) sts. Join without twisting, pm between first and last st.

Ribbing rnd: *K1-tbl, p1; rep from * around. Rep Ribbing rnd until hat measures 1½ inches. Knit 1 rnd. Change to larger needles and MC. Work even in rev St st until hat measures 7 (8) inches.

Shape top
Place 2nd marker after st #40 (44).
Dec rnd: P1, p2tog, purl to 2nd marker, p1, p2tog, purl to end of rnd.
Purl 2 rnds.
Rep last 3 rnds until 12 sts rem, changing to dpn when necessary.
Next rnd: P2tog around. (6 sts)

Cut yarn, leaving an 8-inch end. Draw end through rem sts twice.

Tassel
Cut 2 strands of CC, each 8 inches long; set aside.
Wind CC around cardboard 40 times.
Using 1 reserved strand, tie 1 end; cut opposite end.
Wrap 2nd strand around tassel, about 1 inch below fold. Tie tightly and hide ends in tassel. Trim ends even.
Tie tassel to top of hat.

Wristers

Make 2
Starting at fingers with CC and smaller dpn, cast on 34 (40) sts. Join without twisting, pm between first and last st.
Ribbing rnd: *K1-tbl, p1; rep from * around.
[Rep Ribbing rnd] 5 times.
Change to larger needles and MC. Knit 1 rnd.
Purl 2 (4) rnds, inc 1 st on each side of marker on last rnd. (36, 42 sts)
Thumb opening
Remove marker and work in rows from this point.
Row 1 (RS): Sl 1k wyib, k1, purl to last 2 sts, k2.
Row 2: Sl 1p wyif, p1, knit to last 2 sts, p2.
[Rep Rows 1 and 2] 3 (4) times more.
Replace marker and work in rnds from this point. Purl 2 rnds.
Continue in rev St st, inc 1 st on each side of marker on next rnd. (38, 44 sts)
Work even until wrister measures 7 (8) inches from beg.
Change to CC and smaller needles. Knit 1 rnd.
[Rep Ribbing rnd] 6 times. Bind off in pat. ▪

Family of Socks

Designs by E.J. Slayton

Your whole family will have warm feet when you knit this variety of socks.

Basket-Weave Socks

Skill Level
INTERMEDIATE

Size
Man's small (medium, large) Instructions are given for smallest size, with larger sizes in parentheses. When only 1 number is given, it applies to all sizes.

Finished Measurement
Circumference: Approx 8¼ (9, 9¾) inches

Materials
- Brown Sheep Wildfoote Luxury Sock Yarn 75 percent wool/25 percent nylon fingering weight yarn (215 yds/50g per ball): 2 (2, 3) balls Zane Grey #SY36
- Size 1 (2.25mm) double-pointed needles, or size needed to obtain gauge
- Stitch markers

1 SUPER FINE

Gauge
16 sts and 19 rnds = 2 inches/5cm in St st (blocked)
To save time, take time to check gauge.

Pattern Stitch
Basket Weave (multiple of 6 sts)
Rnds 1 and 2: Knit.
Rnds 3–6: *P4, k2; rep from * around.
Rnds 7 and 8: Knit.
Rnd 9: K3, *p4, k2; rep from * to last 3 sts, p3.
Rnds 10–12: P1, *k2, p4; rep from *, end last rep p3.
Rep Rnds 1–12 for pat.

Sock
Cast on 64 (72, 76) sts.
Join without twisting, pm between first and last st.
Work in k2, p2 ribbing for 2 inches.
Beg pat, inc 2 (0, 2) sts evenly on first rnd. (66, 72, 78 sts)
Work even until top measures 8 inches or desired length.
Knit 2 rnds, dec 2 (0, 2) sts evenly. (64, 72, 76 sts)

Heel
Sl next 32 (36, 38) sts to 1 needle for heel, divide rem 32 (36, 38) sts between 2 needles for instep.
Working in rows on heel sts only, knit across.
Row 1 (WS): Sl 1, purl across.
Row 2: *Sl 1, k1; rep from * across.
Rep Rows 1 and 2 until there are 16 (18, 19) lps on each side of heel flap, ending with Row 2.

Turn heel
Row 1 (WS): Sl 1, p17 (19, 20), p2tog, p1, turn.
Row 2: Sl 1, k5, k2tog, k1, turn.
Row 3: Sl 1, p6, p2tog, p1, turn.
Row 4: Sl 1, k7, k2tog, k1, turn.

Row 5: Sl 1, p8, p2tog, p1, turn.
Row 6: Sl 1, k9, k2tog, k1, turn.
Continue in this manner, working 1 more st before dec each time, until all sts have been worked. (18, 20, 22 sts)

Gusset
Needle 1: Working along right edge of heel flap, with needle containing heel sts, pick up and knit 16 (18, 19) sts (1 st in each lp);
Needle 2: Work instep sts onto 1 needle, *at the same time*, at each end, pick up either a st in the row below, or twist the running thread and knit it tog with the first and last st;
Needle 3: Pick up and knit 16 (18, 19) sts along left edge of heel flap, then knit 9 (10, 11) heel sts onto same needle. There will be 25 (28, 31) sts each on needles 1 and 3, and 32 (36, 38) sts on needle 2. (82, 92, 98 sts)
Rnd 1: Knit.
Rnd 2: Knit to last 3 sts of needle 1, k2tog, k1; knit across needle 2; on needle 3, k1, ssk, knit to end.
Rep Rnds 1 and 2 until needle 1 and needle 3 each contains 16 (18, 19) sts. (64, 72, 76 sts)

Foot
Work even in St st until foot measures approx 2 inches less than desired length.

Toe
Rnd 1: Knit to last 3 sts of needle 1, k2tog, k1; on needle 2, k1, ssk, knit to 3 sts from end, k2tog, k1; on needle 3, k1, ssk, knit to end.
Rnd 2: Knit around.
Rep Rnds 1 and 2 until 28 sts rem, ending with Rnd 1.
With needle 3, knit across sts of needle 1—14 sts on each of 2 needles.

Finishing
Cut yarn, leaving an 18-inch end. Weave toe using Kitchener method.

Three-Color Tweed Socks

Skill Level
■ ■ ■ ▢
INTERMEDIATE

Size
Woman's small (medium, large, extra-large) Instructions are given for smallest size, with larger sizes in parentheses. When only 1 number is given, it applies to all sizes.

Finished Measurement
Circumference: Approx 7½ (8, 9¼, 9¾) inches

Materials
- Brown Sheep Top of the Lamb 100 percent wool sport weight yarn (154 yds/50g per skein): 2 (2, 2, 3) skeins deep forest #352 (MC), 1 skein each russet #200 (A), natural #100 (B)
- Size 3 (3.25mm) set of double-pointed needles or size needed to obtain gauge
- Stitch markers

Gauge
13 sts and 18 rows = 2 inches/5cm in St st
To save time, take time to check gauge.

Pattern Stitch
Three-Color Slip Stitch Tweed
(multiple of 3 sts)
Rnd 1: With A, *k2, sl 1 wyib; rep from * around.
Rnd 2: With A, *p2, sl 1 wyib; rep from * around.
Rnd 3: With B, k1, *sl 1 wyib, k2; rep from * to last 2 sts, end sl 1 wyib, k1.
Rnd 4: With B, p1, *sl 1 wyib, p2; rep from * to last 2 sts, end sl 1 wyib, p1.
Rnd 5: With MC, sl 1, *k2, sl 1 wyib; rep from * to last 2 sts, end k2.
Rnd 6: With MC, sl 1, *p2, sl 1 wyib; rep from * to last 2 sts, end p2.
Rep Rnds 1–6 for pat.

Pattern Note
Sl all sts purlwise, wyib.

Sock
With MC, cast on 48 (52, 60, 64) sts. Join without twisting, mark beg of rnd and work in k2, p2 ribbing until cuff measures 2 inches.
Purl 1 rnd, inc 0 (2, 0, 2) sts evenly. (48, 54, 60, 66 sts)
Work even in pat until cuff measures 7½ inches or desired length from beg, ending with Rnd 6.

Cut A and B.
Knit 1 rnd, dec 0 (2, 0, 2) sts evenly. (48, 52, 60, 64 sts)
Knit across 24 (26, 30, 32) sts with needle 1 (heel sts); divide rem sts so there are 12 (13, 15, 16) sts each on needles 2 and 3 (instep sts). Working on heel sts only, pm in center of flap, after st 12 (13, 15, 16). Shaping will take place evenly on each side of marker.

Heel
Row 1 (WS): Sl 1, purl across.
Row 2: *Sl 1, k1; rep from * across.
Rep Rows 1 and 2 until there are 12 (13, 15, 16) lps on each edge of heel flap, ending with Row 2.

Turn heel
Row 1 (WS): Sl 1, p14 (15, 17, 18), p2tog, p1, turn.
Row 2: Sl 1, k5, k2tog, k1, turn.
Row 3: Sl 1, p6, p2tog, p1, turn.
Row 4: Sl 1, k7, k2tog, k1, turn.
Continue in this manner, working 1 more st

before dec until all sts have been worked.
(14, 16, 18, 18 sts)

Gusset

Needle 1: With needle containing heel sts,
pick up and knit 12 (13, 15, 16) sts in lps along
side of flap;
Needle 2: With free needle, knit 24 (26, 30, 32)
instep sts onto 1 needle, *at the same time,* at
each end, pick up either a st in row below, or
twist running thread and knit it tog with first
and last st;
Needle 3: With free needle, pick up and knit
12 (13, 15, 16) sts in lps along other edge of
heel flap, knit 7 (8, 9, 9) heel sts from needle 1
to needle 3. (62, 68, 78, 82 sts)
Rnd 1: Knit.
Rnd 2: Knit to last 3 sts on needle 1, k2tog, k1;
knit across needle 2; on needle 3, k1, ssk, knit
to end.
[Rep Rnds 1 and 2] 6 (7, 8, 8) times more.
(48, 52, 60, 64 sts)

Foot

Work even in St st until foot measures approx
1¾ inches less than desired length.

Toe

Rnd 1: Knit to last 3 sts of needle 1, k2tog, k1;
on needle 2, k1, ssk, knit to last 3 sts, k2tog, k1;
on needle 3, k1, ssk, knit to end.
Rnd 2: Knit.
Rep Rnds 1 and 2 until 28 sts rem, ending with
Rnd 1.
With needle 3, knit across sts of needle 1–14 sts
on each of 2 needles.

Finishing

Cut yarn, leaving an 18-inch end. Weave toe
using Kitchener method.

Stripes!

Skill Level
INTERMEDIATE

Size
Woman's small (medium, large) Instructions are
given for smallest size, with larger sizes in parentheses. When only 1 number is given, it applies
to all sizes.

Finished Measurement
Circumference: Approx 7 (8, 9) inches

Materials

- Brown Sheep Wildfoote Luxury Sock
  Yarn 75 percent wool/25 percent
  nylon fingering weight yarn (215 yds/50g per
  ball): 2 balls jungle #SY15 (MC), 1 ball each
  temple turquoise #SY19 (A), lullaby #SY34 (B)
- Size 1 (2.25mm) double-pointed needles
  or size needed to obtain gauge
- Stitch markers

Gauge
16 sts and 19 rnds = 2 inches/5cm in St st
(blocked)
To save time, take time to check your gauge.

Pattern Stitch
Stripe Sequence
Work in k2, p2 ribbing of *3 rnds B, 5 rnds A, 8
rnds MC, 5 rnds A; rep from * for desired length.

Sock
With MC, cast on 56 (64, 72) sts. Join without
twisting, pm between first and last st.
Work in k2, p2 ribbing for 2 inches.
Beg stripe sequence and work until top
measures 7 (8, 8) inches or desired length.

Cut A and B, work 2 rnds MC. Work rest of sock in MC.

Heel

Sl next 28 (32, 36) sts to 1 needle for heel, divide rem 28 (32, 36) sts between 2 needles for instep.

Working in rows on heel sts only, knit across.

Row 1 (WS): Sl 1, purl across.

Row 2: *Sl 1, k1; rep from * across.

Rep Rows 1 and 2 until there are 14 (16, 18) lps on each side of heel flap, ending with Row 2.

Turn heel

Row 1 (WS): Sl 1, p15 (17, 19), p2tog, p1, turn.

Row 2: Sl 1, k5, k2tog, k1, turn.

Row 3: Sl 1, p6, p2tog, p1, turn.

Row 4: Sl 1, k7, k2tog, k1, turn.

Row 5: Sl 1, p8, p2tog, p1, turn.

Row 6: Sl 1, k9, k2tog, k1, turn.

Continue in this manner, working 1 more st before dec each time, until all sts have been worked. (16, 18, 20 sts)

Gusset

Needle 1: Working along right edge of heel flap, pick up and k 14 (16, 18) sts (1 st in each loop);

Needle 2: Work instep sts onto 1 needle, *at the same time*, at each end, pick up either a st in the row below, or twist the running thread and knit it tog with the first and last st;

Needle 3: Pick up and knit 14(16, 18) sts along left edge of heel flap, then knit 8 (9, 10) heel sts from needle 1 to needle 3. There will be 22 (25, 28) sts on needles 1 and 3, and 28 (32, 36) sts on needle 2. (72, 82, 92 sts)

Rnd 1: Knit.

Rnd 2: Knit to last 3 sts of needle 1, k2tog, k1; knit sts of needle 2; on needle 3, k1, ssk, knit to end.

Rep Rnds 1 and 2 until needle 1 and needle 3 each contains 14 (16, 18) sts. (56, 64, 72 sts total)

Foot

Work even in St st until foot measures approx 2 inches less than desired length.

Toe

Rnd 1: Knit to last 3 sts of needle 1, k2tog, k1; on needle 2, k1, ssk, knit to last 3 sts, k2tog, k1; on needle 3, k1, ssk, knit to end.

Rnd 2: Knit.

Rep Rnds 1 and 2 until 28 sts rem, ending with Rnd 1.

With needle 3, knit across sts of needle 1. (14 sts on each of 2 needles)

Finishing

Cut yarn, leaving an 18-inch end. Weave toe using Kitchener method.

Wavy Rib Socks

Skill Level

INTERMEDIATE

Size

Child's extra-small (small, medium, large)
Instructions are given for smallest size, with
larger sizes in parentheses. When only
1 number is given, it applies to all sizes.

Finished Measurement

Circumference: 5¼ (6, 6¾, 7½) inches

Materials

- Brown Sheep Wildfoote Luxury Sock
  Yarn 75 percent wool/25 percent
  nylon fingering weight yarn (215 yds/50
  grams per ball): 1 (1, 1, 2) balls columbine
  #SY16 (MC), 1 ball each crystal pink #SY33
  (A), vanilla #SY10 (B), little lilac #SY32 (C)
- Size 1 (2.5mm) double-pointed needles,
  or size needed to obtain gauge
- Stitch markers

1 SUPER FINE

Gauge

16 sts and 19 rnds = 2 inches/5cm in St st
(blocked)
To save time, take time to check your gauge.

Pattern Stitches

Wavy Ribs (multiple of 6 sts)
Rnds 1–4: K2, *p2, k4; rep from * to last 4 sts,
p2, k2.
Rnds 5–8: P1, *k4, p2; rep from * to last 5 sts,
k4, p1.
Rep Rnds 1–8 for pat.

Stripe Sequence

Work *5 rnds A, 6 rnds MC, 3 rnds B, 5 rnds C,
3 rnds B, 6 rnds MC; rep from * for stripe
sequence.

Sock

With MC, cast on 40 (44, 52, 60) sts.
Join without twisting, pm between first and
last st.
Work in k2, p2 ribbing until cuff measures
1½ inches.
Purl 1 rnd, knit 1 rnd inc 2 (4, 2, 0) sts evenly.
(42, 48, 54, 60 sts)
Beg with A, work in pat and stripe sequence
until top measures 4¾ (5½, 6, 6½) inches or
desired length from beg.
Cut all CC, work rem of sock with MC only.
Knit 1 rnd, dec 2 (0, 2, 0) sts evenly. (40, 48,
52, 60 sts)
Knit next rnd, ending 10 (12, 13, 15) sts before
end of rnd.
Knit next 20 (24, 26, 30) sts onto 1 needle for
heel, divide rem 20 (24, 26, 30) sts between
2 needles and leave for instep.

Heel

Working on heel sts only, turn.
Row 1 (WS): Sl 1, purl across.
Row 2: *Sl 1, k1; rep from * across.
Rep Rows 1 and 2 until there are 10 (12, 13, 15)
lps on each side of heel flap, ending with a RS
row, and pm for center of heel after st #10 (12,
13, 15).
Shaping is evenly spaced on each side of marker.

Turn heel

Row 1: Sl 1, p11 (13, 14, 16), p2tog, p1, turn.

Row 2: Sl 1, k5, k2tog, k1, turn.
Row 3: Sl 1, p6, p2tog, p1, turn.
Row 4: Sl 1, k7, k2tog, k1, turn.
Continue in this manner, working 1 more st before dec each time until all sts have been worked. (12, 14, 16, 18 sts)

Gusset

Needle 1: With needle containing heel sts, pick up and knit 10 (12, 13, 15) sts in lps along edge of heel flap;

Needle 2: Work 20 (24, 26, 30) instep sts onto 1 needle, *at the same time*, at each end, pick up either a st in row below, or twist running thread and knit it tog with first and last st; with 3rd needle, pick up and knit 10 (12, 13, 15) sts in lps along other edge of heel flap, k 6 (7, 8, 9) heel sts from needle 1 to needle 3. (52, 62, 68, 78 sts)

Rnd 1: Knit.

Rnd 2: Knit to last 3 sts on needle 1, k2tog, k1; knit across needle 2; on needle 3, k1, ssk, knit to end.

[Rep Rnds 1 and 2] 5 (6, 7,8) times more. (40, 48, 52, 60 sts)

Work even until foot measures 5 (5½, 6, 7) inches or approx 1¾ inches less than desired length.

Toe

Rnd 1: Knit to last 3 sts of needle 1, k2tog, k1; on needle 2, k1, ssk, knit to last 3 sts, k2tog, k1; on needle 3, k1, ssk, knit to end.

Rnd 2: Knit.

Rep Rnds 1 and 2 until 24 sts rem, ending with Rnd 1.

With needle 3, knit across sts of needle 1. (12 sts on each of 2 needles)

Finishing

Cut yarn, leaving an 18-inch end. Weave toe using Kitchener method. ■

Beauty & Her Beast Leg Warmers

Design by Kathy Sasser

Little girls will giggle and tails will wiggle over these fun leg warmers.

Skill Level

EASY

Size

Girl's small (medium, large) or dog's small (medium, large) Instructions are given for smallest size, with larger sizes in parentheses. When only 1 number is given, it applies to all sizes.

Finished Measurements

Girl's Warmers
Length: 9½ (10, 11¼) inches
Bottom width: 9 (10, 11) inches
Top width: 10½ (11½, 12½) inches
Dog's Warmers
Length: 4 (7, 9½) inches
Bottom width: 3½ (4½, 5½) inches
Top width: 4½ (6, 7) inches

Materials

- Brown Sheep Lamb's Pride Superwash Worsted 100 percent wool worsted weight yarn (200 yds/100g per skein): 1 (1, 2) skeins each sea foam #SW16 (A), sweeten pink #SW35 (B) and amethyst #SW62 (C)
- Size 5 (3.75mm) needles
- Size 7 (4.5mm) needles or size needed to obtain gauge

Gauge

20 sts and 26 rows = 4 inches/10cm in St st with larger needles
To save time, take time to check gauge.

Special Abbreviation

MB (Make Bobble): [Purl in front and back of st] twice, purl in front of st again, turn, k5, turn, p5. With LH needle, lift 2nd, 3rd, 4th, then 5th sts one at a time over first st and off needle. Push bobble to RS.

Pattern Stitches

A. 1/1 Rib
Row 1 (RS): K1, *p1, k1; rep from * across.
Row 2: P1, *k1, p1; rep from * across.
Rep Rows 1 and 2 for pat.
B. Color Stripes
Rows 1, 3, 5 and 7 (RS): With C, knit.
Rows 2 and 6: With C, purl.
Row 4: With B p3 (5, 2), *MB, p5; rep from *, end last rep p3 (5, 2).
Rows 8 and 10: With A, purl.
Row 9: With A, knit.
Rep Rows 1–10 for pat.

Pattern Notes

Yarn amounts given are enough to complete 2 sets of leg warmers (one each for beauty and beast)
Girl's leg warmers are designed to fit over pant legs for the following age groups: 4–5 years (6–7 years, 8–9 years)
Bobbles are made on WS rows.

Girl's Leg Warmers

Beg at bottom with smaller needles and A, cast on 45 (51, 55) sts.

Work even in 1/1 Rib for 2 inches, inc 10 (9, 10) sts evenly on last WS row. (55, 60, 65 sts)

Change to larger needles and St st.

Beg with Row 1 (5, 1), work even in Color Stripe pat for 37 (39, 47) rows.

Change to A and smaller needles.

Next row: Purl, dec 4 (3, 2) sts evenly. (51, 57, 63 sts)

Work even in 1/1 Rib for 2 inches.
Bind off loosely.

Finishing

Sew back seam, matching stripes.

Dog Leg Warmers

Beg at bottom with smaller needles and A, cast on 17 (23, 29) sts.

Work even in 1/1 Rib for ¾ (1, 2) inches, inc 10 (12, 14) sts evenly on last WS row. (27, 35, 43 sts)

Change to larger needles and St st.

Work even in Color Stripe pat for 17 (33, 37) rows, changing Row 4 to read as follows: With B p1 (5, 3), *MB, p5; rep from *, end last rep p1 (5, 3).

Change to A and smaller needles.

Next row: Purl, dec 4 (4, 6) sts evenly. (23, 31, 37 sts)

Work even in 1/1 Rib for ¾ (1, 2) inches.
Bind off loosely.

Finishing

Sew back seam, matching stripes. ■

School Spirit Jacket

Design by Kennita Tully

Bold blocks of garter stitch join forces in a show of support for your school.

Skill Level

INTERMEDIATE

Size
Child's 6 (8, 10, 12) Instructions are given for smallest size, with larger sizes in parentheses. When only 1 number is given, it applies to all sizes.

Finished Measurements
Chest: 32 (34, 36, 38) inches
Length: 16 (17, 18, 19) inches

Materials
- Brown Sheep Cotton Fleece 80 percent Pima cotton/20 percent Merino wool worsted weight yarn (215 yds/ 100g per skein): 2 (3, 3, 3) skeins each cavern #CW005 (A) and harvest #CW835 (B)
- Size 5 (3.75mm) straight and 39-inch circular needles or size needed to obtain gauge
- 3 (1-inch) buttons
- Stitch markers

Gauge
20 sts and 40 rows = 4 inches/10cm in garter stitch
20 sts and 24 rows = 4 inches/10cm in St st
To save time, take time to check gauge.

Pattern Stitch
Sleeve Stripe Sequence
Working in St st, work 10 rows A, then 10 rows B.

Pattern Notes
Color blocks are worked in garter st using intarsia method.

Wind separate balls of yarn for each color block. To avoid holes when changing colors, always bring new color up over old.

Back
[With A, cast on 20 (21, 23, 24) sts, with B cast on 20 (21, 23, 24) sts] twice. (80, 84, 92, 96 sts) Knit 40 (42, 46, 48) rows in established color pat.

Next row: [With B k20 (21, 23, 24), with A k20 (21, 23, 24)] twice.

Knit 39 (41, 45, 48) rows in established color pat.

Rep color block pat until 4 rows of blocks have been completed.

Bind off all sts.

Pm for sleeves 6½ (7, 7½, 8) inches from top edge on both sides.

Mark center 5 (5¼, 5¾, 6) inches at top edge for back neck.

Fronts (make 2)

With A, cast on 20 (21, 23, 24) sts, with B cast on 20 (21, 23, 24) sts. (40, 42, 46, 48 sts)

Work even in block pat as for back until 4 rows of blocks have been completed.

Sleeves

With A, pick up and knit 65 (70, 75, 80) sts between markers for sleeves.

Working in Sleeve Stripe pat, dec 1 st each end [every 6th row] 7 (6, 9, 9) times, then [every 4th row] 8 (11, 9, 11) times. (35, 36, 39, 40 sts)

Work even until sleeve measures 12½ (13¾, 14¾, 16½) inches, ending with a knit row.

Do not bind off; p 1 row A.

I-Cord Trim

Cast on 4 sts to LH needle.

*K3, ssk, replace sts just work to LH needle. Rep from * until all sts of sleeve have been worked.

Bind off rem 4 sts.

Assembly

Sew fronts to back, leaving marked center back sts unsewn. Rem sts of front edge will form collar.

Body Trim

Mark top 8 rows of first 3 blocks for button lps. Lps are worked on right edge for girls and left edge for boys.

Beg at side seam with A and circular needle, pick up and knit 1 st in each cast-on or bound-off st and 1 st for every other row around entire opening of garment.

Cast on 4 sts to LH needle.

*K3, ssk, replace sts just work to LH needle. Rep from * until all picked up sts have been worked, working unattached cord for button lp at top of first 3 blocks as follows: [K4, sl sts back to LH needle] 6 times. [Work attached cord to next marker, make button lp] twice, work attached cord until all picked up sts have been worked.

Finishing

Sew last 4 sts to cast-on sts of cord.

Fold front edges of collar back to form collar and tack in place.

Sew sleeves into armholes between markers.

Sew sleeve and side seams. ▪

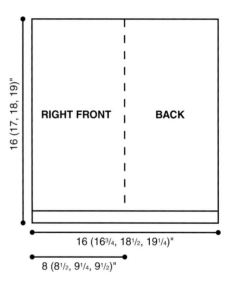

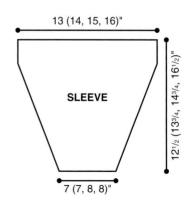

Bold Ribbed Pullover

Design by Kennita Tully

Vibrant stripes combine with ribbing in a colorful kid's pullover.

Skill Level

EASY

Size
Child's 6 (8, 10, 12) Instructions are given for smallest size, with larger sizes in parentheses. When only 1 number is given, it applies to all sizes.

Finished Measurements
Chest: 33 (34½, 36, 38) inches
Length: 17 (18, 19, 20) inches

Materials
• Brown Sheep Cotton Fleece 80 percent Pima cotton/20 percent Merino wool worsted weight yarn (215 yds/100g per skein): 3 (3, 4, 4) skeins raging purple #CW730 (A), 2 (2, 3, 3) skeins blue paradise #CW765 (B) and cherry moon #CW810 (C)
• Size 5 (3.75mm) straight and 16-inch circular needles or size needed to obtain gauge
• Stitch markers
• Stitch holders

Gauge
20 sts and 24 rows = 4 inches/10cm in St st
To save time, take time to check gauge.

Pattern Stitch
Stripes
Row 1 (RS): With A, knit.
Rows 2, 4 and 6: P2, *k2, p2; rep from * across.
Rows 3 and 5: With A, K2, *p2, k2; rep from * across.

Rows 7, 9 and 11: With B, knit.
Rows 8, 10 and 12: With B, purl.
Rows 13–18: Rep Rows 1–6.
Rows 19–24: With C, rep Rows 7–12.
Rep Rows 1–24 for pat.

Back
With A, cast on 82 (86, 90, 94) sts.
Beg with Row 2, work even in Stripes pat until back measures 9½ (10, 10½, 11) inches.
Mark each end st for underarm.
Continue to work even until armhole measures approx 7½ (8, 8½, 9) inches, ending with Row 6, 12, 18 or 24.
Bind off all sts.

Front
Work as for back until armhole measures 4½ (5, 5½, 6) inches, ending with a WS row.
Shape neck
Work across 34 (35, 36, 37) sts, place center 14 (16, 18, 20) sts on holder for front neck, attach 2nd ball of yarn and work across rem 34 (35, 36, 37) sts.
Working on both sides of neck with separate balls of yarn, [dec 1 st at each neck edge every RS row] 7 times. (27, 28, 29, 30 sts on each side of neck)
Work even until armhole measures same as for back.
Bind off all sts.
Sew shoulder seams.

Collar
Beg at left shoulder with RS facing using A and circular needle, pick up and knit 17 sts along

left neck edge, knit across 14 (16, 18, 20) sts on holder, pick up and knit 17 sts along right neck edge, 28 (30, 32, 34) sts along back neck. (76, 80, 84, 88 sts)

Work even in k2, p2 ribbing for 2 inches.

Bind off in pat.

Fold collar to inside and sew loosely to first row of ribbing.

Sleeves

With A, cast on 40 (42, 44, 44) sts.

Work even in k2, p2 ribbing for 7 rows.

Beg with Row 2 work in Stripes pat, inc 1 st each end [every 4th row] 18 (19, 21, 23) times. (76, 80, 86, 90 sts)

Work even until sleeve measures 14½ (15½, 17, 18½) inches.

Bind off.

Assembly

Sew sleeves to body between underarm markers.

Sew sleeve and side seams. ∎

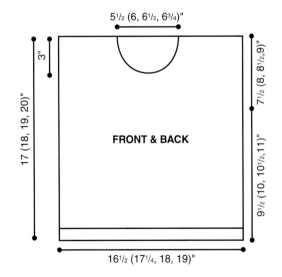

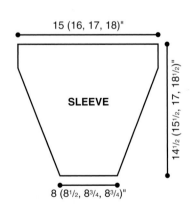

Red, Hot & Blue

Design by E.J. Slayton

Take a simple slip-stitch rib and combine it with bright colors for an easy-to-knit top that will breeze right through the summer weather.

Skill Level
■■□□
EASY

Size
Child's 4 (6, 8, 10) Instructions are given for smallest size, with larger sizes in parentheses. When only 1 number is given, it applies to all sizes.

Finished Measurements
Chest: 26 (28, 30, 32) inches
Length: 13½ (14, 16, 18) inches

Materials
- Brown Sheep Cotton Fleece 80 percent Pima cotton/20 percent merino wool worsted weight yarn (215 yds/100g per skein): 2 (2, 3, 3) skeins barn red #CW201 (MC), 1 skein lapis #CW590 (CC)
- Size 3 (3.25mm) needles
- Size 5 (3.75mm) needles or size needed to obtain gauge
- Stitch holders
- Stitch markers
- Size F/5 (3.75mm) crochet hook
- 1 (½-inch) button

Gauge
20 sts and 28 rows = 4 inches/10cm in St st with larger needles
To save time, take time to check gauge.

Special Abbreviation
M1 (Make 1): Inc by making a backward lp over RH needle.

Pattern Stitch
Slipped Stitch Rib (multiple of 8 sts + 3)
Row 1 (WS): K1, sl 1, k1, *p5, k1, sl 1, k1; rep from * across.
Row 2: Knit.
Rep Rows 1–2 for pat.

Pattern Note
Sl all sts purlwise with yarn in front.

Back
With smaller needles and MC, cast on 65 (69, 73, 81) sts.
Row 1 (WS): P1, *k1, p1; rep from * across.
Row 2: K1, *p1, k1; rep from * across.
Rows 3–11: Rep Rows 1 and 2, ending with Row 1.
Next row: Change to larger needles, knit across, inc 0 (1, 1, 0) st at each edge. (65, 71, 75, 81 sts)
Beg pat (WS): P7 (2, 4, 7), work Row 1 of pat to last 7 (2, 4, 7) sts, purl to end.
Row 2: Knit.
Work in established pat until back measures 8½ (8½, 10, 11½) inches from beg, ending with a WS row.
Shape underarms
Next 2 rows: Bind off 5 (5, 5, 6) sts, work in established pat to end of row. (55, 61, 65, 69 sts)

Dec 1 st each end [every RS row] 4 (4, 5, 5) times by k1, ssk, knit to last 3 sts, end k2tog, k1. (47 53, 55, 59 sts)

Work even until armhole measures 5 (5½, 6, 6½) inches, ending with a WS row.

Shape shoulders

Rows 1 and 2: Bind off 4 (5, 5, 5) sts, work to end of row.

Rows 3 and 4: Bind off 3 (4, 4, 5) sts, work to end of row.

Rows 5 and 6: Bind off 3 (4, 4, 4) sts, work to end of row.

Place rem 27 (27, 29, 31) sts on holder for back neck.

Front

Work as for back until armhole measures 1 (1½, 1½, 2) inches, ending with a WS row.

Beg placket

K21 (24, 25, 27), join 2nd ball of yarn, k5 and place on holder, k21 (24, 25, 27).

Work even in established pat on both sides of neck with separate balls of yarn until armhole measures 3 (3½, 3½, 4) inches, ending with a RS row.

Shape neck

Row 1 (WS): Work in pat across right front; bind off 7 (7, 7, 8) sts at left front neck edge, complete row.

Row 2: Knit across left front sts; bind off 7 (7, 7,

8) sts at right front neck edge, complete row.

Row 3: Work in pat across both sides.

Row 4: Knit to 3 sts from neck edge, k2tog, k1; k1, ssk, knit to end.

[Rep Rows 3 and 4] 3 (3, 4, 4) more times 10 (13, 13, 14) sts rem, *at the same time,* when armhole measures same as back, shape shoulders as for back.

Sleeves

With smaller needles and MC, cast on 45 (49, 53, 57) sts.

Work 9 rows of ribbing as for back.

Knit 1 row.

Beg pat (WS): P5 (7, 1, 3), work Row 1 of pat to last 5 (7, 1, 3) sts, purl to end.

Working in established pat, inc 1 st at each end on next and [every 4th row] 3 (3, 4, 4) times. (51, 55, 61, 65 sts)

Work even until sleeve measures 3½ (3½, 4, 4½) inches from beg, ending with a WS row.

Shape sleeve cap

Bind off 5 (5, 5, 6) sts at beg of next 2 rows. (41, 45, 51, 53 sts)

Dec 1 st at each end [every row] 7 (11, 11, 11) times, then [every other row] 5 (3, 4, 5) times.

Bind off rem 17 (19, 21, 21) sts.

Sew shoulder seams.

Right Front Band

With RS facing, using smaller needles and CC, join yarn and knit across 5 sts from holder, pick up and knit 10 sts along right placket edge, turn.

Row 1 (WS): Sl 1, k8, purl last picked up st tog with 1 st from placket bottom.

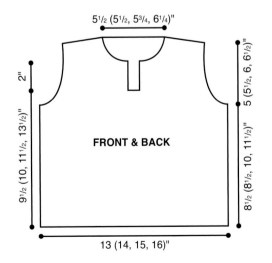

5½ (5½, 5¾, 6¼)"

2"

9½ (10, 11½, 13½)"

FRONT & BACK

5 (5½, 6, 6½)"

8½ (8½, 10, 11½)"

13 (14, 15, 16)"

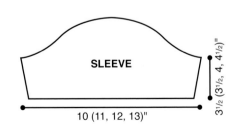

SLEEVE

3½ (3½, 4, 4½)"

10 (11, 12, 13)"

Row 2: Sl 1, k9.
Rows 3 and 4: Rep Rows 1 and 2.
Row 5 (buttonhole): Sl 1, k2tog, yo, ssk, complete as Row 1.

Row 6: Sl 1, k5, [k1, p1] in yo, k2.
Rows 7 and 8: Rep Rows 1 and 2.
Row 9: Rep Row 1.
Sl 1, bind off all sts purlwise.

Left Front Band
Beg at neck edge with smaller needles and CC, pick up and knit 10 sts along left placket edge, turn.
Rows 1–9: Sl 1, k9.
Sl 1, bind off all sts purlwise. Sew lower edge of band to inside bottom of placket.
With crochet hook and B, work 1 sl st in each ridge across top edge of each band. Fasten off.

Collar
With RS facing, using smaller needle and CC, beg at right front neck edge, pick up and knit 7 (7, 7, 8) sts across bound-off sts, pm, pick up and knit 2 sts for every 3 rows along right neck edge, knit 27 (27, 29, 31) back neck sts from holder, pick up and knit sts along left neck edge to match RS, place marker, pick up and knit 7 (7, 7, 8) sts across bound off sts, ending at left front neck edge.
Do not pick up sts in front bands.
Row 1 (WS): Sl 1, knit across.
Row 2: Sl 1, knit to 2 sts before first marker, k2tog, k1, ssk, knit to 3 sts before 2nd marker, k2tog, k1, ssk, knit to end.
Rows 3 and 4: Rep Rows 1 and 2.
Row 5: Sl 1, k1, M1, knit to last 2 sts, M1, k2.
Row 6: Sl 1, knit across.
Rows 7–12: Rep Rows 5 and 6.
Rows 13–16: Sl 1, knit across.
Sl 1, bind off purlwise.

Assembly
Sew sleeves into armholes.
Sew sleeve and side seams.
Sew button opposite buttonhole. ■

Little Gems

Design by Janet Rehfeldt

Jewel colors sparkle like gems on a pullover with a wide size range. Change the colors to a deeper tone for your favorite young man.

Skill Level

INTERMEDIATE

Size

Child's 4 (6, 8, 10, 12) Instructions are given for smallest size, with larger sizes in parentheses. When only 1 number is given, it applies to all sizes.

Finished Measurements

Chest: 29 (31, 33, 35, 37) inches
Sleeve: 11½ (12½, 13½, 15, 16) inches
Total length: 13 (15,16, 17, 18) inches

Materials

- Brown Sheep Lamb's Pride Superwash Bulky 100 percent wool bulky weight yarn (110 yds/100g per skein): 4 (4, 5, 5, 6) skeins white frost #SW11 (MC), 1 skein each serendipity turquoise #SW36 (A) and sweeten pink #SW35 (B), 2 skeins #SW14 saffron (C)

5 BULKY

- Size 9 (5.5mm) 16-inch circular needle
- Size 10 (6mm) needles
- Size 10½ (6.5mm) needles or size needed to obtain gauge
- Stitch holders

Gauge

12 sts and 24 rows = 4 inches/10cm in Gems pat with larger needles
To save time, take time to check gauge.

Pattern Stitch

Gems (uneven number of sts)

Row 1 (RS): With A, k1, *sl 1 wyib, k1; rep from * across.

Row 2: K1, *sl 1 wyif, k1; rep from * across.

Row 3: With MC, knit.

Row 4: Purl.

Row 5: With B, k2, sl 1 wyib, *k1, sl 1 wyib; rep from * to last 2 sts, k2.

Row 6: K2, sl 1 wyif, *k1, sl 1 wyif; rep from * to last 2 sts, k2.

Rows 7–10: With MC, knit.

Row 11: With B, k2, sl 1 wyib, *k1, sl 1 wyib; rep from * to last 2 sts, k2.

Row 12: K2, sl 1 wyif, *k1, sl 1 wyif; rep from * to last 2 sts, k2.

Row 13: With MC, knit.

Row 14: Purl.

Row 15: With A, k1, *sl 1 wyib, k1; rep from * across.

Row 16: K1, *sl 1 wyif, k1; rep from * across.

Rows 17–20: With MC, knit.

Row 21: With A, k1, *sl 1 wyib, k1; rep from * across.

Row 22: K1, *sl 1 wyif, k1; rep from * across.

Row 23: With MC, knit.

Row 24: Purl.

Row 25: With C, k2, sl 1 wyib, *k1, sl 1 wyib; rep from * to last 2 sts, k2.

Row 26: K2, sl 1 wyif, *k1, sl 1 wyif; rep from * to last 2 sts, k2.

Rows 27–30: With MC, knit.

Row 31: With C, k2, sl 1 wyib, *k1, sl 1 wyib; rep from * to last 2 sts, k2.

Row 32: K2, sl 1 wyif, *k1, sl 1 wyif; rep from * to last 2 sts, k2.
Row 33: With MC knit.
Row 34: Purl.
Row 35: With A, k1, *sl 1 wyib; k1; rep from * across.
Row 36: K1, *sl 1 wyif, k1; rep from * across.
Rows 37–40: With MC, knit.
Rep Rows 1–40 for pat.

Pattern Notes

Sl all sts purlwise.
Do not cut MC; carry up along edge.
CC colors are cut after each section of use.

Back

With MC and size 10½ needles, cast on 43 (47, 49, 53, 59) sts.
Knit 1 row.
Work even in Gems pat until back measures approx 5½ (6½, 7, 7½, 8) inches, ending with 2nd row of a CC.
Shape armhole
Bind off 3 sts at beg of next 2 rows. (37, 41, 43, 47, 53 sts)
Work even until armhole measures 5½ (6½, 7, 7½, 8) inches, ending with a WS row.
Shape neck
Work across 10 (11, 11, 13, 14) sts, place next 17 (19, 21, 21, 25) sts on holder, join 2nd ball of yarn and work across rem 10 (11, 11, 13, 14) sts.
Working on both sides of neck with separate balls of yarn, work even until armhole measures 6 (7, 7½, 8, 8½) inches, ending with a WS row.
Bind off all sts with MC.

Bottom Band

With MC and size 10 needles, pick up and knit 37 (41, 43, 47, 53) sts along cast-on edge.
Knit 3 rows.
Change to C and knit 2 rows.
Change to MC and knit 2 rows.
Bind off knitwise on WS.

Front

Work as for back until armhole measures 3 (4, 4½, 5, 5½) inches, ending with a WS row.
Shape neck
Work across 14 (15, 16, 18, 19) sts, place next 9 (11, 11, 11, 15) sts on holder, join 2nd ball of yarn and work across rem 14 (15, 16, 18, 19) sts.
Working on both sides of neck with separate balls of yarn, dec 1 st each side of neck [every other row] 4 (4, 5, 5, 5) times. (10, 11, 11, 13, 14 sts)
Work even until armhole measures same as for back.
Bind off all sts with MC.
Work bottom band as for back.

Sleeves

With MC and size 10½ needles, cast on 23 (23, 25, 25, 27) sts.
Knit 1 row.
Work in Gems pat, inc 1 st each end [every 6th row] 0 (9, 9, 8, 11) times, then [every 7th row] 7 (1, 2, 4, 2) times, working added sts into pat. (37, 43, 47, 49, 53 sts)
Work even until sleeve measures 10 (11, 12, 13½, 14½) inches, ending with a WS row.
Bind off in MC.

Sleeve Band

With MC and size 10 needles, pick up and knit 23 (23, 25, 25, 27) sts along cast-on edge.
Work as for bottom band of back.
Sew shoulder seams.

Collar

Beg at right shoulder with RS facing using MC and size 9 circular needle, pick up and knit 4 sts along right back neck, 17 (19, 21, 21, 25) from back neck holder, 4 sts along left back neck, 12 (14, 14, 16, 16), along left front, 9 (11, 11, 11, 15) from front neck holder, 12 (14, 14, 16, 16) along right front. (58, 66, 68, 72, 80 sts)
Place marker between first and last st.

Work in garter st in following color sequence:
4 rnds MC, 2 rnds C, 4 rnds MC.
Change to C and knit every rnd for 1 inch more.
Bind off loosely.

Assembly

Sew sleeves to body, matching outer top
corners of sleeve to inner corner of armhole shaping, and upper 1 inch of sleeve against bound-off underarm sts.
Sew sleeve and side seams. ▨

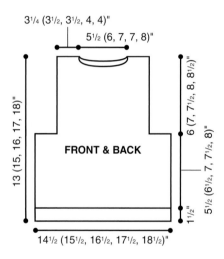

$3\frac{1}{4}$ ($3\frac{1}{2}$, $3\frac{1}{2}$, 4, 4)"

$5\frac{1}{2}$ (6, 7, 7, 8)"

13 (15, 16, 17, 18)"

FRONT & BACK

6 (7, $7\frac{1}{2}$, 8, $8\frac{1}{2}$)"

$5\frac{1}{2}$ ($6\frac{1}{2}$, 7, $7\frac{1}{2}$, 8)"

$1\frac{1}{2}$"

$14\frac{1}{2}$ ($15\frac{1}{2}$, $16\frac{1}{2}$, $17\frac{1}{2}$, $18\frac{1}{2}$)"

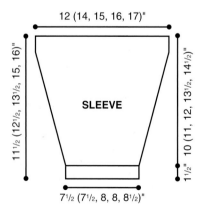

12 (14, 15, 16, 17)"

$11\frac{1}{2}$ ($12\frac{1}{2}$, $13\frac{1}{2}$, 15, 16)"

SLEEVE

10 (11, 12, $13\frac{1}{2}$, $14\frac{1}{2}$)"

$1\frac{1}{2}$"

$7\frac{1}{2}$ ($7\frac{1}{2}$, 8, 8, $8\frac{1}{2}$)"

Rib & Lace Summer Top

Design by Bonnie Franz

An easy lace border trims a refreshing top for girls.

Skill Level

EASY

Size
Girl's small (medium, large, extra-large) To fit size 6 (8, 10, 12) Instructions are given for smallest size, with larger sizes in parentheses. When only 1 number is given, it applies to all sizes.

Finished Measurements
Chest: 27 (30½, 32, 34) inches
Length: 12 (15½, 17½, 19½) inches

Materials
- Brown Sheep Cotton Fleece 80 percent Pima cotton/20 percent Merino wool worsted weight yarn (215 yds/ 100g per skein): 3 (3, 4, 4) skeins spryte #CW640
- Size 11 (8mm) needles

Gauge
12 sts and 15 rows = 4 inches/10cm in 2/2 Rib pat with 3 strands of yarn held tog
To save time, take time to check gauge.

Pattern Stitch
2/2 Rib
Row 1 (RS): K2, *p2, k2; rep from * across.
Row 2: P2, *k2, p2; rep from * across.
Rep Rows 1–2 for pat.

Pattern Notes
Three strands of yarn are held tog for entire garment.
For neatly finished edge, keep each end st at armhole and neck in St st.

Back
With 3 strands held tog, cast on 38 (42, 46, 48) sts.
Border Lace
Rows 1, 3 and 5 (RS): Knit.
Rows 2, 4 and 6: P1, knit to last st, p1.
Row 7: K1, [k1, yo, ssk, k3, k2tog, yo] 4 (5, 5, 5) times, end with:
Size small and large only: K1, yo, ssk, k2.
Size medium only: K1.
Size extra-large only: K1, yo, ssk, k4.
Rows 8, 10 and 12: Purl.
Row 9: K1, [k2, yo, ssk, k1, k2tog, yo, k1] 4 (5, 5, 5) times, end with:
Size small and large only: K2, yo, ssk, k1.
Size medium only: K1.
Size extra-large only: K2, yo, ssk, k3.
Row 11: K1, [k3, yo, sl 1, k2tog, psso, yo, k2] 4 (5, 5, 5) times, end with:
Size small and large only: K5.
Size medium only: K1.
Size extra-large only: K3, yo, sl 1, k2tog, psso, yo, k1.
Rows 13–18: Rep Rows 1–6.
Change to 2/2 Rib and work even until back measures 7 (9, 10½, 12) inches.

Shape armhole

Bind off 3 (3, 4, 4) sts at beg of next 2 rows. (32, 36, 38, 40 sts)
Dec 1 st each end [every other row] 4 times. (24, 28, 30, 32 sts)
Work even until armhole measures 4 (5½, 6, 6½) inches, ending with a WS row.

Shape shoulders and back neck

Bind off 1 (2, 3, 2) sts at beg of next 2 rows, then 2 (2, 2, 3) sts at beg of following 4 rows.
Bind off rem 14 (16, 16, 16) sts for back neck.

Front

Work as for back until armhole measures 1½ (2½, 3, 3½) inches, ending with a WS row.

Shape neck

Work across 8 (9, 10, 11) sts, join 2nd ball of yarn and bind off next 8 (10, 10, 10) sts for neck, work to end of row.
Working on both sides of neck with separate balls of yarn, dec 1 st at each neck edge [every other row] 3 times. (5, 6, 7, 8 sts)
Work even until armhole measures same as for back.
Shape shoulders as for back.

Assembly

Sew shoulder and side seams. ■

Special Thanks

We would like to thank Brown Sheep Co. for providing all the yarn used in this book. We also appreciate the help provided by Peggy Jo Wells and the Brown Sheep staff throughout the publishing process. It's been great working with them. We also thank the talented knitting designers whose work is featured in this collection.

Laura Andersson
Texture Time, 133

Diane Elliott
October's Glory, 138

Nazanin S. Fard
Lovely Evening Scarf, 136

Bonnie Franz
Chunky Turtleneck Tunic, 6
My Dog & Me, 44
Rainbow Poncho, 66
Rib & Lace Summer Top, 173

Shari Haux
Daisy Stitch Pullover, 9

Katharine Hunt
Comfy Cozy Hoodie, 74
Evening Heather Poncho, 69
Rugged Sleeveless Jacket, 56

Melissa Leapman
Dappled Forest Glen, 32
Intertwined Cables, 16
Quick Cherry Tee, 116
Textured Stripes, 103

Cindy Polfer
Jade Stripes Jacket, 98
Sideways Stripes, 78

Sandi Prosser
Autumn Harvest, 20
Checkered Cardi, 82
Coral Lace Shell, 120
Purple Passion, 12
Summer Berry Shell, 106
Summer Confection, 124

Janet Rehfeldt
Little Gems, 169

Kathy Sasser
Beauty & Her Beast Leg Warmers, 156

Jean Schafer-Albers
Fair Isle Basket-Weave Jacket, 94

Pauline Schultz
Rodeo Vest, 60

E.J. Slayton
Family of Socks, 149
Red, Hot & Blue, 165

Colleen Smitherman
Checkered Denim Scarf, 144
Lovely Lace Turtleneck, 40
My Blue Heaven, 112

Scarlet Taylor
Day & Night Ensemble, 48
Favorite Teen Turtleneck, 52
Flirty in Lime, 86
Slipped-Stitch Casual Pullover, 127

Kennita Tully
Bold Ribbed Pullover, 162
Checks & Stripes Twin Set, 35
Easy Zoom Jacket, 63
School Spirit Jacket, 159
Silk Cabled Shell, 109

Barbara Venishnick
Autumn Elegance, 90
Purple Pop Over, 24

Lois S. Young
Fun in the Sun, 130

Diane Zangl
Bubblegum Hat & Wristers, 146
Jaunty Stripes Hat & Scarf, 141
Monterey Bay, 27

Standard Abbreviations

[ ] work instructions within brackets as many times as directed
( ) work instructions within parentheses in the place directed
** repeat instructions following the asterisks as directed
* repeat instructions following the single asterisk as directed
" inch(es)
approx approximately
beg begin/beginning
CC contrasting color
ch chain stitch
cm centimeter(s)
cn cable needle
dec decrease/decreases/decreasing
dpn double-pointed needle(s)
g gram
inc increase/increases/increasing
k knit
k2tog knit 2 stitches together

LH left hand
lp(s) loop(s)
m meter(s)
M1 make one stitch
MC main color
mm millimeter(s)
oz ounce(s)
p purl
pat(s) pattern(s)
pm place marker
p2tog purl 2 stitches together
psso pass slipped stitch over
rem remain/remaining
rep repeat(s)
rev St st reverse stockinette stitch
RH right hand
rnd(s) rounds
RS right side
skp slip, knit, pass stitch over—one stitch decreased

sk2p slip 1, knit 2 together, pass slip stitch over the knit 2 together; 2 stitches have been decreased
sl slip
sl 1k slip 1 knitwise
sl 1p slip 1 purlwise
sl st slip stitch(es)
ssk slip, slip, knit these 2 stitches together— a decrease
st(s) stitch(es)
St st stockinette stitch/ stocking stitch
tbl through back loop(s)
tog together
WS wrong side
wyib with yarn in back
wyif with yarn in front
yd(s) yard(s)
yfwd yarn forward
yo yarn over